C-170   CAREER EXAMINATION SERIES

*This is your
PASSBOOK for...*

Court Attendant/ Security Officer

*Test Preparation Study Guide
Questions & Answers*

COPYRIGHT NOTICE

This book is SOLELY intended for, is sold ONLY to, and its use is RESTRICTED to individual, bona fide applicants or candidates who qualify by virtue of having seriously filed applications for appropriate license, certificate, professional and/or promotional advancement, higher school matriculation, scholarship, or other legitimate requirements of education and/or governmental authorities.

This book is NOT intended for use, class instruction, tutoring, training, duplication, copying, reprinting, excerption, or adaptation, etc., by:

1) Other publishers
2) Proprietors and/or Instructors of "Coaching" and/or Preparatory Courses
3) Personnel and/or Training Divisions of commercial, industrial, and governmental organizations
4) Schools, colleges, or universities and/or their departments and staffs, including teachers and other personnel
5) Testing Agencies or Bureaus
6) Study groups which seek by the purchase of a single volume to copy and/or duplicate and/or adapt this material for use by the group as a whole without having purchased individual volumes for each of the members of the group
7) Et al.

Such persons would be in violation of appropriate Federal and State statutes.

PROVISION OF LICENSING AGREEMENTS – Recognized educational, commercial, industrial, and governmental institutions and organizations, and others legitimately engaged in educational pursuits, including training, testing, and measurement activities, may address request for a licensing agreement to the copyright owners, who will determine whether, and under what conditions, including fees and charges, the materials in this book may be used them. In other words, a licensing facility exists for the legitimate use of the material in this book on other than an individual basis. However, it is asseverated and affirmed here that the material in this book CANNOT be used without the receipt of the express permission of such a licensing agreement from the Publishers. Inquiries re licensing should be addressed to the company, attention rights and permissions department.

All rights reserved, including the right of reproduction in whole or in part, in any form or by any means, electronic or mechanical, including photocopying, recording, or by any information storage and retrieval system, without permission in writing from the Publisher.

Copyright © 2025 by
National Learning Corporation

212 Michael Drive, Syosset, NY 11791
(516) 921-8888 • www.passbooks.com
E-mail: info@passbooks.com

PASSBOOK® SERIES

THE *PASSBOOK® SERIES* has been created to prepare applicants and candidates for the ultimate academic battlefield – the examination room.

At some time in our lives, each and every one of us may be required to take an examination – for validation, matriculation, admission, qualification, registration, certification, or licensure.

Based on the assumption that every applicant or candidate has met the basic formal educational standards, has taken the required number of courses, and read the necessary texts, the *PASSBOOK® SERIES* furnishes the one special preparation which may assure passing with confidence, instead of failing with insecurity. Examination questions – together with answers – are furnished as the basic vehicle for study so that the mysteries of the examination and its compounding difficulties may be eliminated or diminished by a sure method.

This book is meant to help you pass your examination provided that you qualify and are serious in your objective.

The entire field is reviewed through the huge store of content information which is succinctly presented through a provocative and challenging approach – the question-and-answer method.

A climate of success is established by furnishing the correct answers at the end of each test.

You soon learn to recognize types of questions, forms of questions, and patterns of questioning. You may even begin to anticipate expected outcomes.

You perceive that many questions are repeated or adapted so that you can gain acute insights, which may enable you to score many sure points.

You learn how to confront new questions, or types of questions, and to attack them confidently and work out the correct answers.

You note objectives and emphases, and recognize pitfalls and dangers, so that you may make positive educational adjustments.

Moreover, you are kept fully informed in relation to new concepts, methods, practices, and directions in the field.

You discover that you are actually taking the examination all the time: you are preparing for the examination by "taking" an examination, not by reading extraneous and/or supererogatory textbooks.

In short, this PASSBOOK®, used directedly, should be an important factor in helping you to pass your test.

COURT ATTENDANT/SECURITY OFFICER

DISTINGUISHING FEATURES OF THE CLASS:
The work involves responsibility for maintaining order and security in and around courtroom complexes and judges' offices. The work also involves maintaining order and decorum in the courtroom; ensuring protection of judges, juries, witnesses, and other participants; and controlling and ensuring protection of the general public in and around courtroom areas. Work is carried out in accordance with well-established, standard security procedures as well as the special procedures imposed by the judge sitting at the time. Work is performed under the direct supervision of the Court Security Supervisor with some leeway allowed the incumbent for the exercise of independent judgment in carrying out duties as long as they are performed within established guidelines and according to standard operating procedures. Supervision of subordinates is usually not a feature of this class of positions. Does related work as required.

SUBJECTS OF EXAMINATION:
The written test is designed to evaluate knowledge, skills, and/or abilities in the following areas:
1. **Applying written information (laws, rules, regulations, procedures, etc.) in civil law enforcement and court-related situations** - These questions test how well you can apply written information, in the form of rules, to given situations similar to those typically encountered by civil law enforcement employees, court attendants, and court security officers. All information needed to answer the questions is contained in the rules, regulations, etc., which are cited.
2. **Following directions (maps)** - These questions test your ability to follow physical/geographic directions using street maps or building maps. You will have to read and understand a set of directions and then use them on a simple map.
3. **Preparing written material** - These questions test for the ability to present information clearly and accurately, and to organize paragraphs logically and comprehensibly. For some questions, you will be given information in two or three sentences followed by four restatements of the information. You must then choose the best version. For other questions, you will be given paragraphs with their sentences out of order. You must then choose, from four suggestions, the best order for the sentences.
4. **Public contact principles and practices** - These questions test for knowledge of techniques used to interact with other people, to gather and present information, and to provide assistance, advice, and effective customer service in a courteous and professional manner. Questions will cover such topics as understanding and responding to people with diverse needs, perspectives, personalities, and levels of familiarity with agency operations, as well as acting in a way that both serves the public and reflects well on your agency.

HOW TO TAKE A TEST

I. YOU MUST PASS AN EXAMINATION

A. WHAT EVERY CANDIDATE SHOULD KNOW

Examination applicants often ask us for help in preparing for the written test. What can I study in advance? What kinds of questions will be asked? How will the test be given? How will the papers be graded?

As an applicant for a civil service examination, you may be wondering about some of these things. Our purpose here is to suggest effective methods of advance study and to describe civil service examinations.

Your chances for success on this examination can be increased if you know how to prepare. Those "pre-examination jitters" can be reduced if you know what to expect. You can even experience an adventure in good citizenship if you know why civil service exams are given.

B. WHY ARE CIVIL SERVICE EXAMINATIONS GIVEN?

Civil service examinations are important to you in two ways. As a citizen, you want public jobs filled by employees who know how to do their work. As a job seeker, you want a fair chance to compete for that job on an equal footing with other candidates. The best-known means of accomplishing this two-fold goal is the competitive examination.

Exams are widely publicized throughout the nation. They may be administered for jobs in federal, state, city, municipal, town or village governments or agencies.

Any citizen may apply, with some limitations, such as the age or residence of applicants. Your experience and education may be reviewed to see whether you meet the requirements for the particular examination. When these requirements exist, they are reasonable and applied consistently to all applicants. Thus, a competitive examination may cause you some uneasiness now, but it is your privilege and safeguard.

C. HOW ARE CIVIL SERVICE EXAMS DEVELOPED?

Examinations are carefully written by trained technicians who are specialists in the field known as "psychological measurement," in consultation with recognized authorities in the field of work that the test will cover. These experts recommend the subject matter areas or skills to be tested; only those knowledges or skills important to your success on the job are included. The most reliable books and source materials available are used as references. Together, the experts and technicians judge the difficulty level of the questions.

Test technicians know how to phrase questions so that the problem is clearly stated. Their ethics do not permit "trick" or "catch" questions. Questions may have been tried out on sample groups, or subjected to statistical analysis, to determine their usefulness.

Written tests are often used in combination with performance tests, ratings of training and experience, and oral interviews. All of these measures combine to form the best-known means of finding the right person for the right job.

II. HOW TO PASS THE WRITTEN TEST

A. NATURE OF THE EXAMINATION

To prepare intelligently for civil service examinations, you should know how they differ from school examinations you have taken. In school you were assigned certain definite pages to read or subjects to cover. The examination questions were quite detailed and usually emphasized memory. Civil service exams, on the other hand, try to discover your present ability to perform the duties of a position, plus your potentiality to learn these duties. In other words, a civil service exam attempts to predict how successful you will be. Questions cover such a broad area that they cannot be as minute and detailed as school exam questions.

In the public service similar kinds of work, or positions, are grouped together in one "class." This process is known as *position-classification*. All the positions in a class are paid according to the salary range for that class. One class title covers all of these positions, and they are all tested by the same examination.

B. FOUR BASIC STEPS

1) Study the announcement

How, then, can you know what subjects to study? Our best answer is: "Learn as much as possible about the class of positions for which you've applied." The exam will test the knowledge, skills and abilities needed to do the work.

Your most valuable source of information about the position you want is the official exam announcement. This announcement lists the training and experience qualifications. Check these standards and apply only if you come reasonably close to meeting them.

The brief description of the position in the examination announcement offers some clues to the subjects which will be tested. Think about the job itself. Review the duties in your mind. Can you perform them, or are there some in which you are rusty? Fill in the blank spots in your preparation.

Many jurisdictions preview the written test in the exam announcement by including a section called "Knowledge and Abilities Required," "Scope of the Examination," or some similar heading. Here you will find out specifically what fields will be tested.

2) Review your own background

Once you learn in general what the position is all about, and what you need to know to do the work, ask yourself which subjects you already know fairly well and which need improvement. You may wonder whether to concentrate on improving your strong areas or on building some background in your fields of weakness. When the announcement has specified "some knowledge" or "considerable knowledge," or has used adjectives like "beginning principles of…" or "advanced … methods," you can get a clue as to the number and difficulty of questions to be asked in any given field. More questions, and hence broader coverage, would be included for those subjects which are more important in the work. Now weigh your strengths and weaknesses against the job requirements and prepare accordingly.

3) Determine the level of the position

Another way to tell how intensively you should prepare is to understand the level of the job for which you are applying. Is it the entering level? In other words, is this the position in which beginners in a field of work are hired? Or is it an intermediate or advanced level? Sometimes this is indicated by such words as "Junior" or "Senior" in the class title. Other jurisdictions use Roman numerals to designate the level – Clerk I, Clerk II, for example. The word "Supervisor" sometimes appears in the title. If the level is not indicated by the title, check the description of duties. Will you be working under very close supervision, or will you have responsibility for independent decisions in this work?

4) Choose appropriate study materials

Now that you know the subjects to be examined and the relative amount of each subject to be covered, you can choose suitable study materials. For beginning level jobs, or even advanced ones, if you have a pronounced weakness in some aspect of your training, read a modern, standard textbook in that field. Be sure it is up to date and has general coverage. Such books are normally available at your library, and the librarian will be glad to help you locate one. For entry-level positions, questions of appropriate difficulty are chosen – neither highly advanced questions, nor those too simple. Such questions require careful thought but not advanced training.

If the position for which you are applying is technical or advanced, you will read more advanced, specialized material. If you are already familiar with the basic principles of your field, elementary textbooks would waste your time. Concentrate on advanced textbooks and technical periodicals. Think through the concepts and review difficult problems in your field.

These are all general sources. You can get more ideas on your own initiative, following these leads. For example, training manuals and publications of the government agency which employs workers in your field can be useful, particularly for technical and professional positions. A letter or visit to the government department involved may result in more specific study suggestions, and certainly will provide you with a more definite idea of the exact nature of the position you are seeking.

III. KINDS OF TESTS

Tests are used for purposes other than measuring knowledge and ability to perform specified duties. For some positions, it is equally important to test ability to make adjustments to new situations or to profit from training. In others, basic mental abilities not dependent on information are essential. Questions which test these things may not appear as pertinent to the duties of the position as those which test for knowledge and information. Yet they are often highly important parts of a fair examination. For very general questions, it is almost impossible to help you direct your study efforts. What we can do is to point out some of the more common of these general abilities needed in public service positions and describe some typical questions.

1) General information

Broad, general information has been found useful for predicting job success in some kinds of work. This is tested in a variety of ways, from vocabulary lists to questions about current events. Basic background in some field of work, such as sociology or economics, may be sampled in a group of questions. Often these are principles which have become familiar to most persons through exposure rather than through formal training. It is difficult to advise you how to study for these questions; being alert to the world around you is our best suggestion.

2) Verbal ability

An example of an ability needed in many positions is verbal or language ability. Verbal ability is, in brief, the ability to use and understand words. Vocabulary and grammar tests are typical measures of this ability. Reading comprehension or paragraph interpretation questions are common in many kinds of civil service tests. You are given a paragraph of written material and asked to find its central meaning.

3) **Numerical ability**

Number skills can be tested by the familiar arithmetic problem, by checking paired lists of numbers to see which are alike and which are different, or by interpreting charts and graphs. In the latter test, a graph may be printed in the test booklet which you are asked to use as the basis for answering questions.

4) **Observation**

A popular test for law-enforcement positions is the observation test. A picture is shown to you for several minutes, then taken away. Questions about the picture test your ability to observe both details and larger elements.

5) **Following directions**

In many positions in the public service, the employee must be able to carry out written instructions dependably and accurately. You may be given a chart with several columns, each column listing a variety of information. The questions require you to carry out directions involving the information given in the chart.

6) **Skills and aptitudes**

Performance tests effectively measure some manual skills and aptitudes. When the skill is one in which you are trained, such as typing or shorthand, you can practice. These tests are often very much like those given in business school or high school courses. For many of the other skills and aptitudes, however, no short-time preparation can be made. Skills and abilities natural to you or that you have developed throughout your lifetime are being tested.

Many of the general questions just described provide all the data needed to answer the questions and ask you to use your reasoning ability to find the answers. Your best preparation for these tests, as well as for tests of facts and ideas, is to be at your physical and mental best. You, no doubt, have your own methods of getting into an exam-taking mood and keeping "in shape." The next section lists some ideas on this subject.

IV. KINDS OF QUESTIONS

Only rarely is the "essay" question, which you answer in narrative form, used in civil service tests. Civil service tests are usually of the short-answer type. Full instructions for answering these questions will be given to you at the examination. But in case this is your first experience with short-answer questions and separate answer sheets, here is what you need to know:

1) Multiple-choice Questions

Most popular of the short-answer questions is the "multiple choice" or "best answer" question. It can be used, for example, to test for factual knowledge, ability to solve problems or judgment in meeting situations found at work.

A multiple-choice question is normally one of three types—

- It can begin with an incomplete statement followed by several possible endings. You are to find the one ending which *best* completes the statement, although some of the others may not be entirely wrong.
- It can also be a complete statement in the form of a question which is answered by choosing one of the statements listed.

- It can be in the form of a problem – again you select the best answer.

Here is an example of a multiple-choice question with a discussion which should give you some clues as to the method for choosing the right answer:

When an employee has a complaint about his assignment, the action which will *best* help him overcome his difficulty is to
    A. discuss his difficulty with his coworkers
    B. take the problem to the head of the organization
    C. take the problem to the person who gave him the assignment
    D. say nothing to anyone about his complaint

In answering this question, you should study each of the choices to find which is best. Consider choice "A" – Certainly an employee may discuss his complaint with fellow employees, but no change or improvement can result, and the complaint remains unresolved. Choice "B" is a poor choice since the head of the organization probably does not know what assignment you have been given, and taking your problem to him is known as "going over the head" of the supervisor. The supervisor, or person who made the assignment, is the person who can clarify it or correct any injustice. Choice "C" is, therefore, correct. To say nothing, as in choice "D," is unwise. Supervisors have and interest in knowing the problems employees are facing, and the employee is seeking a solution to his problem.

2) True/False Questions

The "true/false" or "right/wrong" form of question is sometimes used. Here a complete statement is given. Your job is to decide whether the statement is right or wrong.

SAMPLE: A roaming cell-phone call to a nearby city costs less than a non-roaming call to a distant city.

This statement is wrong, or false, since roaming calls are more expensive.

This is not a complete list of all possible question forms, although most of the others are variations of these common types. You will always get complete directions for answering questions. Be sure you understand *how* to mark your answers – ask questions until you do.

V. RECORDING YOUR ANSWERS

Computer terminals are used more and more today for many different kinds of exams.
For an examination with very few applicants, you may be told to record your answers in the test booklet itself. Separate answer sheets are much more common. If this separate answer sheet is to be scored by machine – and this is often the case – it is highly important that you mark your answers correctly in order to get credit.
An electronic scoring machine is often used in civil service offices because of the speed with which papers can be scored. Machine-scored answer sheets must be marked with a pencil, which will be given to you. This pencil has a high graphite content which responds to the electronic scoring machine. As a matter of fact, stray dots may register as answers, so do not let your pencil rest on the answer sheet while you are pondering the correct answer. Also, if your pencil lead breaks or is otherwise defective, ask for another.

Since the answer sheet will be dropped in a slot in the scoring machine, be careful not to bend the corners or get the paper crumpled.

The answer sheet normally has five vertical columns of numbers, with 30 numbers to a column. These numbers correspond to the question numbers in your test booklet. After each number, going across the page are four or five pairs of dotted lines. These short dotted lines have small letters or numbers above them. The first two pairs may also have a "T" or "F" above the letters. This indicates that the first two pairs only are to be used if the questions are of the true-false type. If the questions are multiple choice, disregard the "T" and "F" and pay attention only to the small letters or numbers.

Answer your questions in the manner of the sample that follows:

32. The largest city in the United States is
    A. Washington, D.C.
    B. New York City
    C. Chicago
    D. Detroit
    E. San Francisco

1) Choose the answer you think is best. (New York City is the largest, so "B" is correct.)
2) Find the row of dotted lines numbered the same as the question you are answering. (Find row number 32)
3) Find the pair of dotted lines corresponding to the answer. (Find the pair of lines under the mark "B.")
4) Make a solid black mark between the dotted lines.

VI. BEFORE THE TEST

Common sense will help you find procedures to follow to get ready for an examination. Too many of us, however, overlook these sensible measures. Indeed, nervousness and fatigue have been found to be the most serious reasons why applicants fail to do their best on civil service tests. Here is a list of reminders:

- Begin your preparation early – Don't wait until the last minute to go scurrying around for books and materials or to find out what the position is all about.
- Prepare continuously – An hour a night for a week is better than an all-night cram session. This has been definitely established. What is more, a night a week for a month will return better dividends than crowding your study into a shorter period of time.
- Locate the place of the exam – You have been sent a notice telling you when and where to report for the examination. If the location is in a different town or otherwise unfamiliar to you, it would be well to inquire the best route and learn something about the building.
- Relax the night before the test – Allow your mind to rest. Do not study at all that night. Plan some mild recreation or diversion; then go to bed early and get a good night's sleep.
- Get up early enough to make a leisurely trip to the place for the test – This way unforeseen events, traffic snarls, unfamiliar buildings, etc. will not upset you.
- Dress comfortably – A written test is not a fashion show. You will be known by number and not by name, so wear something comfortable.

- Leave excess paraphernalia at home – Shopping bags and odd bundles will get in your way. You need bring only the items mentioned in the official notice you received; usually everything you need is provided. Do not bring reference books to the exam. They will only confuse those last minutes and be taken away from you when in the test room.
- Arrive somewhat ahead of time – If because of transportation schedules you must get there very early, bring a newspaper or magazine to take your mind off yourself while waiting.
- Locate the examination room – When you have found the proper room, you will be directed to the seat or part of the room where you will sit. Sometimes you are given a sheet of instructions to read while you are waiting. Do not fill out any forms until you are told to do so; just read them and be prepared.
- Relax and prepare to listen to the instructions
- If you have any physical problem that may keep you from doing your best, be sure to tell the test administrator. If you are sick or in poor health, you really cannot do your best on the exam. You can come back and take the test some other time.

VII. AT THE TEST

The day of the test is here and you have the test booklet in your hand. The temptation to get going is very strong. Caution! There is more to success than knowing the right answers. You must know how to identify your papers and understand variations in the type of short-answer question used in this particular examination. Follow these suggestions for maximum results from your efforts:

1) Cooperate with the monitor

The test administrator has a duty to create a situation in which you can be as much at ease as possible. He will give instructions, tell you when to begin, check to see that you are marking your answer sheet correctly, and so on. He is not there to guard you, although he will see that your competitors do not take unfair advantage. He wants to help you do your best.

2) Listen to all instructions

Don't jump the gun! Wait until you understand all directions. In most civil service tests you get more time than you need to answer the questions. So don't be in a hurry. Read each word of instructions until you clearly understand the meaning. Study the examples, listen to all announcements and follow directions. Ask questions if you do not understand what to do.

3) Identify your papers

Civil service exams are usually identified by number only. You will be assigned a number; you must not put your name on your test papers. Be sure to copy your number correctly. Since more than one exam may be given, copy your exact examination title.

4) Plan your time

Unless you are told that a test is a "speed" or "rate of work" test, speed itself is usually not important. Time enough to answer all the questions will be provided, but this does not mean that you have all day. An overall time limit has been set. Divide the total time (in minutes) by the number of questions to determine the approximate time you have for each question.

5) Do not linger over difficult questions

If you come across a difficult question, mark it with a paper clip (useful to have along) and come back to it when you have been through the booklet. One caution if you do this – be sure to skip a number on your answer sheet as well. Check often to be sure that you have not lost your place and that you are marking in the row numbered the same as the question you are answering.

6) Read the questions

Be sure you know what the question asks! Many capable people are unsuccessful because they failed to *read* the questions correctly.

7) Answer all questions

Unless you have been instructed that a penalty will be deducted for incorrect answers, it is better to guess than to omit a question.

8) Speed tests

It is often better NOT to guess on speed tests. It has been found that on timed tests people are tempted to spend the last few seconds before time is called in marking answers at random – without even reading them – in the hope of picking up a few extra points. To discourage this practice, the instructions may warn you that your score will be "corrected" for guessing. That is, a penalty will be applied. The incorrect answers will be deducted from the correct ones, or some other penalty formula will be used.

9) Review your answers

If you finish before time is called, go back to the questions you guessed or omitted to give them further thought. Review other answers if you have time.

10) Return your test materials

If you are ready to leave before others have finished or time is called, take ALL your materials to the monitor and leave quietly. Never take any test material with you. The monitor can discover whose papers are not complete, and taking a test booklet may be grounds for disqualification.

VIII. EXAMINATION TECHNIQUES

1) Read the general instructions carefully. These are usually printed on the first page of the exam booklet. As a rule, these instructions refer to the timing of the examination; the fact that you should not start work until the signal and must stop work at a signal, etc. If there are any *special* instructions, such as a choice of questions to be answered, make sure that you note this instruction carefully.

2) When you are ready to start work on the examination, that is as soon as the signal has been given, read the instructions to each question booklet, underline any key words or phrases, such as *least, best, outline, describe* and the like. In this way you will tend to answer as requested rather than discover on reviewing your paper that you *listed without describing*, that you selected the *worst* choice rather than the *best* choice, etc.

3) If the examination is of the objective or multiple-choice type – that is, each question will also give a series of possible answers: A, B, C or D, and you are called upon to select the best answer and write the letter next to that answer on your answer paper – it is advisable to start answering each question in turn. There may be anywhere from 50 to 100 such questions in the three or four hours allotted and you can see how much time would be taken if you read through all the questions before beginning to answer any. Furthermore, if you come across a question or group of questions which you know would be difficult to answer, it would undoubtedly affect your handling of all the other questions.

4) If the examination is of the essay type and contains but a few questions, it is a moot point as to whether you should read all the questions before starting to answer any one. Of course, if you are given a choice – say five out of seven and the like – then it is essential to read all the questions so you can eliminate the two that are most difficult. If, however, you are asked to answer all the questions, there may be danger in trying to answer the easiest one first because you may find that you will spend too much time on it. The best technique is to answer the first question, then proceed to the second, etc.

5) Time your answers. Before the exam begins, write down the time it started, then add the time allowed for the examination and write down the time it must be completed, then divide the time available somewhat as follows:
    - If 3-1/2 hours are allowed, that would be 210 minutes. If you have 80 objective-type questions, that would be an average of 2-1/2 minutes per question. Allow yourself no more than 2 minutes per question, or a total of 160 minutes, which will permit about 50 minutes to review.
    - If for the time allotment of 210 minutes there are 7 essay questions to answer, that would average about 30 minutes a question. Give yourself only 25 minutes per question so that you have about 35 minutes to review.

6) The most important instruction is to *read each question* and make sure you know what is wanted. The second most important instruction is to *time yourself properly* so that you answer every question. The third most important instruction is to *answer every question*. Guess if you have to but include something for each question. Remember that you will receive no credit for a blank and will probably receive some credit if you write something in answer to an essay question. If you guess a letter – say "B" for a multiple-choice question – you may have guessed right. If you leave a blank as an answer to a multiple-choice question, the examiners may respect your feelings but it will not add a point to your score. Some exams may penalize you for wrong answers, so in such cases *only*, you may not want to guess unless you have some basis for your answer.

7) Suggestions
    a. Objective-type questions
        1. Examine the question booklet for proper sequence of pages and questions
        2. Read all instructions carefully
        3. Skip any question which seems too difficult; return to it after all other questions have been answered
        4. Apportion your time properly; do not spend too much time on any single question or group of questions

5. Note and underline key words – *all, most, fewest, least, best, worst, same, opposite*, etc.
6. Pay particular attention to negatives
7. Note unusual option, e.g., unduly long, short, complex, different or similar in content to the body of the question
8. Observe the use of "hedging" words – *probably, may, most likely*, etc.
9. Make sure that your answer is put next to the same number as the question
10. Do not second-guess unless you have good reason to believe the second answer is definitely more correct
11. Cross out original answer if you decide another answer is more accurate; do not erase until you are ready to hand your paper in
12. Answer all questions; guess unless instructed otherwise
13. Leave time for review

b. Essay questions
1. Read each question carefully
2. Determine exactly what is wanted. Underline key words or phrases.
3. Decide on outline or paragraph answer
4. Include many different points and elements unless asked to develop any one or two points or elements
5. Show impartiality by giving pros and cons unless directed to select one side only
6. Make and write down any assumptions you find necessary to answer the questions
7. Watch your English, grammar, punctuation and choice of words
8. Time your answers; don't crowd material

8) Answering the essay question

Most essay questions can be answered by framing the specific response around several key words or ideas. Here are a few such key words or ideas:

M's: manpower, materials, methods, money, management
P's: purpose, program, policy, plan, procedure, practice, problems, pitfalls, personnel, public relations

a. Six basic steps in handling problems:
1. Preliminary plan and background development
2. Collect information, data and facts
3. Analyze and interpret information, data and facts
4. Analyze and develop solutions as well as make recommendations
5. Prepare report and sell recommendations
6. Install recommendations and follow up effectiveness

b. Pitfalls to avoid
1. *Taking things for granted* – A statement of the situation does not necessarily imply that each of the elements is necessarily true; for example, a complaint may be invalid and biased so that all that can be taken for granted is that a complaint has been registered

2. *Considering only one side of a situation* – Wherever possible, indicate several alternatives and then point out the reasons you selected the best one
3. *Failing to indicate follow up* – Whenever your answer indicates action on your part, make certain that you will take proper follow-up action to see how successful your recommendations, procedures or actions turn out to be
4. *Taking too long in answering any single question* – Remember to time your answers properly

IX. AFTER THE TEST

Scoring procedures differ in detail among civil service jurisdictions although the general principles are the same. Whether the papers are hand-scored or graded by machine we have described, they are nearly always graded by number. That is, the person who marks the paper knows only the number – never the name – of the applicant. Not until all the papers have been graded will they be matched with names. If other tests, such as training and experience or oral interview ratings have been given, scores will be combined. Different parts of the examination usually have different weights. For example, the written test might count 60 percent of the final grade, and a rating of training and experience 40 percent. In many jurisdictions, veterans will have a certain number of points added to their grades.

After the final grade has been determined, the names are placed in grade order and an eligible list is established. There are various methods for resolving ties between those who get the same final grade – probably the most common is to place first the name of the person whose application was received first. Job offers are made from the eligible list in the order the names appear on it. You will be notified of your grade and your rank as soon as all these computations have been made. This will be done as rapidly as possible.

People who are found to meet the requirements in the announcement are called "eligibles." Their names are put on a list of eligible candidates. An eligible's chances of getting a job depend on how high he stands on this list and how fast agencies are filling jobs from the list.

When a job is to be filled from a list of eligibles, the agency asks for the names of people on the list of eligibles for that job. When the civil service commission receives this request, it sends to the agency the names of the three people highest on this list. Or, if the job to be filled has specialized requirements, the office sends the agency the names of the top three persons who meet these requirements from the general list.

The appointing officer makes a choice from among the three people whose names were sent to him. If the selected person accepts the appointment, the names of the others are put back on the list to be considered for future openings.

That is the rule in hiring from all kinds of eligible lists, whether they are for typist, carpenter, chemist, or something else. For every vacancy, the appointing officer has his choice of any one of the top three eligibles on the list. This explains why the person whose name is on top of the list sometimes does not get an appointment when some of the persons lower on the list do. If the appointing officer chooses the second or third eligible, the No. 1 eligible does not get a job at once, but stays on the list until he is appointed or the list is terminated.

X. HOW TO PASS THE INTERVIEW TEST

The examination for which you applied requires an oral interview test. You have already taken the written test and you are now being called for the interview test – the final part of the formal examination.

You may think that it is not possible to prepare for an interview test and that there are no procedures to follow during an interview. Our purpose is to point out some things you can do in advance that will help you and some good rules to follow and pitfalls to avoid while you are being interviewed.

What is an interview supposed to test?

The written examination is designed to test the technical knowledge and competence of the candidate; the oral is designed to evaluate intangible qualities, not readily measured otherwise, and to establish a list showing the relative fitness of each candidate – as measured against his competitors – for the position sought. Scoring is not on the basis of "right" and "wrong," but on a sliding scale of values ranging from "not passable" to "outstanding." As a matter of fact, it is possible to achieve a relatively low score without a single "incorrect" answer because of evident weakness in the qualities being measured.

Occasionally, an examination may consist entirely of an oral test – either an individual or a group oral. In such cases, information is sought concerning the technical knowledges and abilities of the candidate, since there has been no written examination for this purpose. More commonly, however, an oral test is used to supplement a written examination.

Who conducts interviews?

The composition of oral boards varies among different jurisdictions. In nearly all, a representative of the personnel department serves as chairman. One of the members of the board may be a representative of the department in which the candidate would work. In some cases, "outside experts" are used, and, frequently, a businessman or some other representative of the general public is asked to serve. Labor and management or other special groups may be represented. The aim is to secure the services of experts in the appropriate field.

However the board is composed, it is a good idea (and not at all improper or unethical) to ascertain in advance of the interview who the members are and what groups they represent. When you are introduced to them, you will have some idea of their backgrounds and interests, and at least you will not stutter and stammer over their names.

What should be done before the interview?

While knowledge about the board members is useful and takes some of the surprise element out of the interview, there is other preparation which is more substantive. It *is* possible to prepare for an oral interview – in several ways:

1) Keep a copy of your application and review it carefully before the interview

This may be the only document before the oral board, and the starting point of the interview. Know what education and experience you have listed there, and the sequence and dates of all of it. Sometimes the board will ask you to review the highlights of your experience for them; you should not have to hem and haw doing it.

2) Study the class specification and the examination announcement

Usually, the oral board has one or both of these to guide them. The qualities, characteristics or knowledges required by the position sought are stated in these documents. They offer valuable clues as to the nature of the oral interview. For example, if the job involves supervisory responsibilities, the announcement will usually indicate that knowledge of modern supervisory methods and the qualifications of the candidate as a supervisor will be tested. If so, you can expect such questions, frequently in the form of a hypothetical situation which you are expected to solve. NEVER go into an oral without knowledge of the duties and responsibilities of the job you seek.

3) Think through each qualification required

Try to visualize the kind of questions you would ask if you were a board member. How well could you answer them? Try especially to appraise your own knowledge and background in each area, *measured against the job sought*, and identify any areas in which you are weak. Be critical and realistic – do not flatter yourself.

4) Do some general reading in areas in which you feel you may be weak

For example, if the job involves supervision and your past experience has NOT, some general reading in supervisory methods and practices, particularly in the field of human relations, might be useful. Do NOT study agency procedures or detailed manuals. The oral board will be testing your understanding and capacity, not your memory.

5) Get a good night's sleep and watch your general health and mental attitude

You will want a clear head at the interview. Take care of a cold or any other minor ailment, and of course, no hangovers.

What should be done on the day of the interview?

Now comes the day of the interview itself. Give yourself plenty of time to get there. Plan to arrive somewhat ahead of the scheduled time, particularly if your appointment is in the fore part of the day. If a previous candidate fails to appear, the board might be ready for you a bit early. By early afternoon an oral board is almost invariably behind schedule if there are many candidates, and you may have to wait. Take along a book or magazine to read, or your application to review, but leave any extraneous material in the waiting room when you go in for your interview. In any event, relax and compose yourself.

The matter of dress is important. The board is forming impressions about you – from your experience, your manners, your attitude, and your appearance. Give your personal appearance careful attention. Dress your best, but not your flashiest. Choose conservative, appropriate clothing, and be sure it is immaculate. This is a business interview, and your appearance should indicate that you regard it as such. Besides, being well groomed and properly dressed will help boost your confidence.

Sooner or later, someone will call your name and escort you into the interview room. *This is it*. From here on you are on your own. It is too late for any more preparation. But remember, you asked for this opportunity to prove your fitness, and you are here because your request was granted.

What happens when you go in?

The usual sequence of events will be as follows: The clerk (who is often the board stenographer) will introduce you to the chairman of the oral board, who will introduce you to the other members of the board. Acknowledge the introductions before you sit down. Do not be surprised if you find a microphone facing you or a stenotypist sitting by. Oral interviews are usually recorded in the event of an appeal or other review.

Usually the chairman of the board will open the interview by reviewing the highlights of your education and work experience from your application – primarily for the benefit of the other members of the board, as well as to get the material into the record. Do not interrupt or comment unless there is an error or significant misinterpretation; if that is the case, do not hesitate. But do not quibble about insignificant matters. Also, he will usually ask you some question about your education, experience or your present job – partly to get you to start talking and to establish the interviewing "rapport." He may start the actual questioning, or turn it over to one of the other members. Frequently, each member undertakes the questioning on a particular area, one in which he is perhaps most competent, so you can expect each member to participate in the examination. Because time is limited, you may also expect some rather abrupt switches in the direction the questioning takes, so do not be upset by it. Normally, a board member will not pursue a single line of questioning unless he discovers a particular strength or weakness.

After each member has participated, the chairman will usually ask whether any member has any further questions, then will ask you if you have anything you wish to add. Unless you are expecting this question, it may floor you. Worse, it may start you off on an extended, extemporaneous speech. The board is not usually seeking more information. The question is principally to offer you a last opportunity to present further qualifications or to indicate that you have nothing to add. So, if you feel that a significant qualification or characteristic has been overlooked, it is proper to point it out in a sentence or so. Do not compliment the board on the thoroughness of their examination – they have been sketchy, and you know it. If you wish, merely say, "No thank you, I have nothing further to add." This is a point where you can "talk yourself out" of a good impression or fail to present an important bit of information. Remember, *you close the interview yourself*.

The chairman will then say, "That is all, Mr. _____, thank you." Do not be startled; the interview is over, and quicker than you think. Thank him, gather your belongings and take your leave. Save your sigh of relief for the other side of the door.

How to put your best foot forward

Throughout this entire process, you may feel that the board individually and collectively is trying to pierce your defenses, seek out your hidden weaknesses and embarrass and confuse you. Actually, this is not true. They are obliged to make an appraisal of your qualifications for the job you are seeking, and they want to see you in your best light. Remember, they must interview all candidates and a non-cooperative candidate may become a failure in spite of their best efforts to bring out his qualifications. Here are 15 suggestions that will help you:

1) Be natural – Keep your attitude confident, not cocky

If you are not confident that you can do the job, do not expect the board to be. Do not apologize for your weaknesses, try to bring out your strong points. The board is interested in a positive, not negative, presentation. Cockiness will antagonize any board member and make him wonder if you are covering up a weakness by a false show of strength.

2) Get comfortable, but don't lounge or sprawl

Sit erectly but not stiffly. A careless posture may lead the board to conclude that you are careless in other things, or at least that you are not impressed by the importance of the occasion. Either conclusion is natural, even if incorrect. Do not fuss with your clothing, a pencil or an ashtray. Your hands may occasionally be useful to emphasize a point; do not let them become a point of distraction.

3) Do not wisecrack or make small talk

This is a serious situation, and your attitude should show that you consider it as such. Further, the time of the board is limited – they do not want to waste it, and neither should you.

4) Do not exaggerate your experience or abilities

In the first place, from information in the application or other interviews and sources, the board may know more about you than you think. Secondly, you probably will not get away with it. An experienced board is rather adept at spotting such a situation, so do not take the chance.

5) If you know a board member, do not make a point of it, yet do not hide it

Certainly you are not fooling him, and probably not the other members of the board. Do not try to take advantage of your acquaintanceship – it will probably do you little good.

6) Do not dominate the interview

Let the board do that. They will give you the clues – do not assume that you have to do all the talking. Realize that the board has a number of questions to ask you, and do not try to take up all the interview time by showing off your extensive knowledge of the answer to the first one.

7) Be attentive

You only have 20 minutes or so, and you should keep your attention at its sharpest throughout. When a member is addressing a problem or question to you, give him your undivided attention. Address your reply principally to him, but do not exclude the other board members.

8) Do not interrupt

A board member may be stating a problem for you to analyze. He will ask you a question when the time comes. Let him state the problem, and wait for the question.

9) Make sure you understand the question

Do not try to answer until you are sure what the question is. If it is not clear, restate it in your own words or ask the board member to clarify it for you. However, do not haggle about minor elements.

10) Reply promptly but not hastily

A common entry on oral board rating sheets is "candidate responded readily," or "candidate hesitated in replies." Respond as promptly and quickly as you can, but do not jump to a hasty, ill-considered answer.

11) Do not be peremptory in your answers

A brief answer is proper – but do not fire your answer back. That is a losing game from your point of view. The board member can probably ask questions much faster than you can answer them.

12) Do not try to create the answer you think the board member wants

He is interested in what kind of mind you have and how it works – not in playing games. Furthermore, he can usually spot this practice and will actually grade you down on it.

13) Do not switch sides in your reply merely to agree with a board member

Frequently, a member will take a contrary position merely to draw you out and to see if you are willing and able to defend your point of view. Do not start a debate, yet do not surrender a good position. If a position is worth taking, it is worth defending.

14) Do not be afraid to admit an error in judgment if you are shown to be wrong

The board knows that you are forced to reply without any opportunity for careful consideration. Your answer may be demonstrably wrong. If so, admit it and get on with the interview.

15) Do not dwell at length on your present job

The opening question may relate to your present assignment. Answer the question but do not go into an extended discussion. You are being examined for a *new* job, not your present one. As a matter of fact, try to phrase ALL your answers in terms of the job for which you are being examined.

Basis of Rating

Probably you will forget most of these "do's" and "don'ts" when you walk into the oral interview room. Even remembering them all will not ensure you a passing grade. Perhaps you did not have the qualifications in the first place. But remembering them will help you to put your best foot forward, without treading on the toes of the board members.

Rumor and popular opinion to the contrary notwithstanding, an oral board wants you to make the best appearance possible. They know you are under pressure – but they also want to see how you respond to it as a guide to what your reaction would be under the pressures of the job you seek. They will be influenced by the degree of poise you display, the personal traits you show and the manner in which you respond.

ABOUT THIS BOOK

This book contains tests divided into Examination Sections. Go through each test, answering every question in the margin. We have also attached a sample answer sheet at the back of the book that can be removed and used. At the end of each test look at the answer key and check your answers. On the ones you got wrong, look at the right answer choice and learn. Do not fill in the answers first. Do not memorize the questions and answers, but understand the answer and principles involved. On your test, the questions will likely be different from the samples. Questions are changed and new ones added. If you understand these past questions you should have success with any changes that arise. Tests may consist of several types of questions. We have additional books on each subject should more study be advisable or necessary for you. Finally, the more you study, the better prepared you will be. This book is intended to be the last thing you study before you walk into the examination room. Prior study of relevant texts is also recommended. NLC publishes some of these in our Fundamental Series. Knowledge and good sense are important factors in passing your exam. Good luck also helps. So now study this Passbook, absorb the material contained within and take that knowledge into the examination. Then do your best to pass that exam.

EXAMINATION SECTION

EXAMINATION SECTION
TEST 1

DIRECTIONS: Each question or incomplete statement is followed by several suggested answers or completions. Select the one that BEST answers the question or completes the statement. *PRINT THE LETTER OF THE CORRECT ANSWER IN THE SPACE AT THE RIGHT.*

1. Physical and mental health are essential to the officer. According to this statement, the officer MUST be

    A. as wise as he is strong
    B. smarter than most people
    C. sound in mind and body
    D. stronger than the average criminal

2. Teamwork is the basis of successful law enforcement. The factor stressed by this statement is

    A. cooperation   B. determination
    C. initiative   D. pride

3. Legal procedure is a means, not an end. Its function is merely to accomplish the enforcement of legal rights.
   A litigant has no vested interest in the observance of the rules of procedure as such. All that he should be entitled to demand is that he be given an opportunity for a fair and impartial trial of his case. He should not be permitted to invoke the aid of technical rules merely to embarrass his adversary.
   According to this paragraph, it is MOST correct to state that

    A. observance of the rules of procedure guarantees a fair trial
    B. embarrassment of an adversary through technical rules does not make a fair trial
    C. a litigant is not interested in the observance of rules of procedure
    D. technical rules must not be used in a trial

4. One theory states that all criminal behavior is taught by a process of communication within small intimate groups. An individual engages in criminal behavior if the number of criminal patterns which he has acquired exceed the number of non-criminal patterns. This statement indicates that criminal behavior is

    A. learned   B. instinctive
    C. hereditary   D. reprehensible

5. The law enforcement staff of today requires training and mental qualities of a high order. The poorly or partially prepared staff member lowers the standard of work, retards his own earning power, and fails in a career meant to provide a livelihood and social improvement.
   According to this statement,

    A. an inefficient member of a law enforcement staff will still earn a good livelihood
    B. law enforcement officers move in good social circles
    C. many people fail in law enforcement careers
    D. persons of training and ability are essential to a law enforcement staff

6. In any state, no crime can occur unless there is a written law forbidding the act or the omission in question; and even though an act may not be exactly in harmony with public policy, such act is not a crime unless it is expressly forbidden by legislative statement.
According to the above statement,
   A. a crime is committed with reference to a particular law
   B. acts not in harmony with public policy should be forbidden by law
   C. non-criminal activity will promote public welfare
   D. legislative enactments frequently forbid actions in harmony with public policy

7. The unrestricted sale of firearms is one of the main causes of our shameful crime record.
According to this statement, one of the causes of our crime record is
   A. development of firepower
   B. ease of securing weapons
   C. increased skill in using guns
   D. scientific perfection of firearms

8. Every person must be informed of the reason for his arrest unless he is arrested in the actual commission of a crime. Sufficient force to effect the arrest may be used, but the courts frown on brutal methods.
According to this statement, a person does not have to be informed of the reason for his arrest if
   A. brutal force was not used in effecting it
   B. the courts will later turn the defendant loose
   C. the person arrested knows force will be used if necessary
   D. the reason for it is clearly evident from the circumstances

9. An important duty of an officer is to keep order in the court.
On the basis of this statement, it is PROBABLY true that
   A. it is more important for an officer to be strong than it is for him to be smart
   B. people involved in court trials are noisy if not kept in check
   C. not every duty of an officer is important
   D. the maintenance of order is important for the proper conduct of court business

10. Ideally, a correctional system should include several types of institutions to provide different degrees of custody.
On the basis of this statement, one could MOST reasonably say that
   A. as the number of institutions in a correctional system increases, the efficiency of the system increases
   B. the difference in degree of custody for the inmate depends on the types of institutions in a correctional system
   C. the greater the variety of institutions, the stricter the degree of custody that can be maintained
   D. the same type of correctional institution is not desirable for the custody of all prisoners

11. The enforced idleness of a large percentage of adult men and women in our prisons is one of the direct causes of the tensions which burst forth in riot and disorder.
    On the basis of this statement, a good reason why inmates should perform daily work of some kind is that

    A. better morale and discipline can be maintained when inmates are kept busy
    B. daily work is an effective way of punishing inmates for the crimes they have committed
    C. law-abiding citizens must work, therefore labor should also be required of inmates
    D. products of inmates' labor will in part pay the cost of their maintenance

12. With industry invading rural areas, the use of the automobile, and the speed of modern communications and transportation, the problems of neglect and delinquency are no longer peculiar to cities but an established feature of everyday life.
    This statement implies MOST directly that

    A. delinquents are moving from cities to rural areas
    B. delinquency and neglect are found in rural areas
    C. delinquency is not as much of a problem in rural areas as in cities
    D. rural areas now surpass cities in industry

13. Young men from minority groups, if unable to find employment, become discouraged and hopeless because of their economic position and may finally resort to any means of supplying their wants.
    The MOST reasonable of the following conclusions that may be drawn from this statement only is that

    A. discouragement sometimes leads to crime
    B. in general, young men from minority groups are criminals
    C. unemployment turns young men from crime
    D. young men from minority groups are seldom employed

14. To prevent crime, we must deal with the possible criminal long before he reaches the prison. Our aim should be not merely to reform the law breakers but to strike at the roots of crime: neglectful parents, bad companions, unsatisfactory homes, selfishness, disregard for the rights of others, and bad social conditions.
    The above statement recommends

    A. abolition of prisons
    B. better reformatories
    C. compulsory education
    D. general social reform

15. There is evidence which shows that comic books which glorify the criminal and criminal acts have a distinct influence in producing young criminals.
    According to this statement,

    A. comic books affect the development of criminal careers
    B. comic books specialize in reporting criminal acts
    C. young criminals read comic books exclusively
    D. young criminals should not be permitted to read comic books

16. Suppose a study shows that juvenile delinquents are equal in intelligence but three school grades behind juvenile non-delinquents.
    On the basis of this information only, it is MOST reasonable to say that

    A. a delinquent usually progresses to the educational limit set by his intelligence
    B. educational achievement depends on intelligence only
    C. educational achievement is closely associated with delinquency
    D. lack of intelligence is closely associated with delinquency

17. There is no proof today that the experience of a prison sentence makes a better citizen of an adult. On the contrary, there seems some evidence that the experience is an unwholesome one that frequently confirms the criminality of the inmate.
    From the above paragraph only, it may be BEST concluded that

    A. prison sentences tend to punish rather than rehabilitate
    B. all criminals should be given prison sentences
    C. we should abandon our penal institutions
    D. penal institutions are effective in rehabilitating criminals

18. Some courts are referred to as *criminal* courts while others are known as *civil* courts. This distinction in name is MOST probably based on the

    A. historical origin of the court
    B. link between the court and the police
    C. manner in which the judges are chosen
    D. type of cases tried there

19. Many children who are exposed to contacts and experiences of a delinquent nature become educated and trained in crime in the course of participating in the daily life of the neighborhood.
    From this statement only, we may reasonably conclude that

    A. delinquency passes from parent to child
    B. neighborhood influences are usually bad
    C. schools are training grounds for delinquents
    D. none of the above conclusions is reasonable

20. Old age insurance, for whose benefits a quarter of a million city employees may elect to become eligible, is one feature of the Social Security Act that is wholly administered by the Federal government.
    On the basis of this paragraph only, it may MOST reasonably be inferred that

    A. a quarter of a million city employees are drawing old age insurance
    B. a quarter of a million city employees have elected to become eligible for old age insurance
    C. the city has no part in administering Social Security old age insurance
    D. only the Federal government administers the Social Security Act

21. An officer's revolver is a defensive, and not offensive, weapon.
    On the basis of this statement only, an officer should BEST draw his revolver to

    A. fire at an unarmed burglar
    B. force a suspect to confess
    C. frighten a juvenile delinquent
    D. protect his own life

22. Prevention of crime is of greater value to the community than the punishment of crime. 22.____
    If this statement is accepted as true, GREATEST emphasis should be placed on

    A. malingering   B. medication
    C. imprisonment   D. rehabilitation

23. The criminal is rarely or never reformed. Acceptance of this statement as true would 23.____
    mean that GREATEST emphasis should be placed on

    A. imprisonment   B. parole
    C. probation   D. malingering

24. The MOST accurate of the following statements about persons convicted of crimes is 24.____
    that

    A. their criminal behavior is almost invariably the result of low intelligence
    B. they are almost invariably legally insane
    C. they are more likely to come from underprivileged groups than from other groups
    D. they have certain facial characteristics which distinguish them from non-criminals

25. Suppose a study shows that the I.Q. (Intelligence Quotient) of prison inmates is 95 as 25.____
    opposed to an I.Q. of 100 for a numerically equivalent civilian group.
    A claim, on the basis of this study, that criminals have a lower I.Q. than non-criminals
    would be

    A. *improper;* prison inmates are criminals who have been caught
    B. *proper;* the study was numerically well done
    C. *improper;* the sample was inadequate
    D. *proper;* even misdemeanors are sometimes penalized by prison sentences

Questions 26-45.

   DIRECTIONS: Select the number of the word or expression that MOST NEARLY expresses
               the meaning of the capitalized word in the group.

26. ABDUCT   26.____

    A. lead   B. kidnap   C. sudden   D. worthless

27. BIAS   27.____

    A. ability   B. envy   C. prejudice   D. privilege

28. COERCE   28.____

    A. cancel   B. force   C. rescind   D. rugged

29. CONDONE   29.____

    A. combine   B. pardon   C. revive   D. spice

30. CONSISTENCY   30.____

    A. bravery   B. readiness
    C. strain   D. uniformity

31. **CREDENCE**
    - A. belief
    - B. devotion
    - C. resemblance
    - D. tempo

32. **CURRENT**
    - A. backward
    - B. brave
    - C. prevailing
    - D. wary

33. **CUSTODY**
    - A. advisement
    - B. belligerence
    - C. guardianship
    - D. suspicion

34. **DEBILITY**
    - A. deceitfulness
    - B. decency
    - C. strength
    - D. weakness

35. **DEPLETE**
    - A. beg
    - B. empty
    - C. excuse
    - D. fold

36. **ENUMERATE**
    - A. name one by one
    - B. disappear
    - C. get rid of
    - D. pretend

37. **FEIGN**
    - A. allow
    - B. incur
    - C. pretend
    - D. weaken

38. **INSTIGATE**
    - A. analyze
    - B. coordinate
    - C. oppose
    - D. provoke

39. **LIABLE**
    - A. careless
    - B. growing
    - C. mistaken
    - D. responsible

40. **PONDER**
    - A. attack
    - B. heavy
    - C. meditate
    - D. solicit

41. **PUGILIST**
    - A. farmer
    - B. politician
    - C. prize fighter
    - D. stage actor

42. **QUELL**
    - A. explode
    - B. inform
    - C. shake
    - D. suppress

43. **RECIPROCAL**
    - A. mutual
    - B. organized
    - C. redundant
    - D. thoughtful

44. RUSE

    A. burn   B. impolite   C. rot   D. trick

45. STEALTHY

    A. crazed   B. flowing   C. sly   D. wicked

Questions 46-50.

DIRECTIONS: Each of the sentences in Questions 46 through 50 may be classified under one of the following four categories:
- A. faulty because of incorrect grammar
- B. faulty because of incorrect punctuation
- C. faulty because of incorrect capitalization or incorrect spelling
- D. correct

Examine each sentence carefully to determine under which of the above four options it is best classified. Then, in the space at the right, print the capital letter preceding the option which is the BEST of the four suggested above. Each faulty sentence contains but one type of error. Consider a sentence to be correct if it contains none of the types of errors mentioned, even though there may be other correct ways of expressing the same thought.

46. They told both he and I that the prisoner had escaped.

47. Any superior officer, who, disregards the just complaints of his subordinates, is remiss in the performance of his duty.

48. Only those members of the national organization who resided in the Middle west attended the conference in Chicago.

49. We told him to give the investigation assignment to whoever was available.

50. Please do not disappoint and embarass us by not appearing in court.

KEY (CORRECT ANSWERS)

1. C	11. A	21. D	31. A	41. C
2. A	12. B	22. D	32. C	42. D
3. B	13. A	23. A	33. C	43. A
4. A	14. D	24. C	34. D	44. D
5. D	15. A	25. A	35. B	45. C
6. A	16. C	26. B	36. A	46. A
7. B	17. A	27. C	37. C	47. B
8. D	18. D	28. B	38. D	48. C
9. D	19. D	29. B	39. D	49. D
10. D	20. C	30. D	40. C	50. C

TEST 2

DIRECTIONS: Each question or incomplete statement is followed by several suggested answers or completions. Select the one that BEST answers the question or completes the statement. *PRINT THE LETTER OF THE CORRECT ANSWER IN THE SPACE AT THE RIGHT.*

1. Suppose a man falls from a two-story high scaffold and is unconscious. You should

    A. call for medical assistance and avoid moving the man
    B. get someone to help you move him indoors to a bed
    C. have someone help you walk him around until he revives
    D. hold his head up and pour a stimulant down his throat

    1.____

2. For proper first aid treatment, a person who has fainted should be

    A. doused with cold water and then warmly covered
    B. given artificial respiration until he is revived
    C. laid down with his head lower than the rest of his body
    D. slapped on the face until he is revived

    2.____

3. If you are called on to give first aid to a person who is suffering from shock, you should

    A. apply cold towels
    B. give him a stimulant
    C. keep him awake
    D. wrap him warmly

    3.____

4. Artificial respiration would NOT be proper first aid for a person suffering from

    A. drowning
    B. electric shock
    C. external bleeding
    D. suffocation

    4.____

5. Suppose you are called on to give first aid to several victims of an accident. First attention should be given to the one who is

    A. bleeding severely
    B. groaning loudly
    C. unconscious
    D. vomiting

    5.____

6. If an officer's weekly salary is increased from $480 to $540, then the percent of increase is _____ percent.

    A. 10   B. 11 1/9   C. 12 1/2   D. 20

    6.____

7. Suppose that one-half the officers in a department have served for more than ten years and one-third have served for more than 15 years.
   Then, the fraction of officers who have served between ten and fifteen years is

    A. 1/3   B. 1/5   C. 1/6   D. 1/12

    7.____

8. In a city prison there are four floors on which prisoners are housed. The top floor houses one-quarter of the inmates, the bottom floor houses one-sixth of the inmates, one-third are housed on the second floor. The rest of the inmates are housed on the third floor. If there are 90 inmates housed on the third floor, the TOTAL number of inmates housed on all four floors together is

    A. 270   B. 360   C. 450   D. 540

    8.____

9. Suppose that ten percent of those who commit serious crimes are convicted and that fifteen percent of those convicted are sentenced for more than 3 years.
   The percentage of those committing serious crimes who are sentenced for more than 3 years is _____ percent.

   A. 15   B. 1.5   C. .15   D. .015

10. Assume that there are 1,100 employees in a city agency. Of these, 15 percent are officers, 80 percent of whom are attorneys; of the attorneys, two-fifths have been with the agency over five years.
    Then, the number of officers who are attorneys and have over five years experience with the agency is MOST NEARLY

    A. 45   B. 53   C. 132   D. 165

11. An employee who has 500 cartons of supplies to pack can pack them at the rate of 50 an hour. After this employee has worked for 1/2 hour, he is joined by another employee who can pack 45 cartons an hour.
    Assuming that both employees can maintain their respective rates of speed, then the TOTAL number of hours required to pack all the cartons is

    A. 4 1/2   B. 5   C. 5 1/2   D. 6 1/2

12. Thirty-six officers can complete an assignment in 22 days. Assuming that all officers work at the same rate of speed, the number of officers that would be needed to complete this assignment in 12 days is

    A. 42   B. 54   C. 66   D. 72

Questions 13-15.

DIRECTIONS: Questions 13 through 15 are to be answered on the basis of the table below. Data for certain categories have been omitted from the table. You are to calculate the missing numbers if needed to answer the questions.

	2007	2008	Numerical Increase
Correction Officers	1,226	1,347	
Court Officers		529	34
Deputy Sheriffs	38	40	
Supervisors			
	2,180	2,414	

13. The number in the *Supervisors* group in 2007 was MOST NEARLY

    A. 500   B. 475   C. 450   D. 425

14. The LARGEST percentage increase from 2007 to 2008 was in the group of

    A. Correction Officers   B. Court Officers
    C. Deputy Sheriffs   D. Supervisors

15. In 2008, the ratio of the number of Correction Officers to the total of the other three categories of employees was MOST NEARLY

    A. 1:1   B. 2:1   C. 3:1   D. 4:1

16. A directed verdict is made by a court when

    A. the facts are not disputed
    B. the defendant's motion for a directed verdict has been denied
    C. there is no question of law involved
    D. neither party has moved for a directed verdict

17. Papers on appeal of a criminal case do NOT include one of the following:

    A. Summons
    B. Minutes of trial
    C. Complaint
    D. Intermediate motion papers

18. A pleading titled *Smith vs. Jones, et al* indicates

    A. two plaintiffs
    B. two defendants
    C. more than two defendants
    D. unknown defendants

19. A District Attorney makes a *prima facie* case when

    A. there is proof of guilt beyond a reasonable doubt
    B. the evidence is sufficient to convict in the absence of rebutting evidence
    C. the prosecution presents more evidence than the defense
    D. the defendant fails to take the stand

20. A person is NOT qualified to act as a trial juror in a criminal action if he or she

    A. has been convicted previously of a misdemeanor
    B. is under 18 years of age
    C. has scruples against the death penalty
    D. does not own property of a value at least $500

21. A court clerk who falsifies a court record commits a(n)

    A. misdemeanor
    B. offense
    C. felony
    D. no crime, but automatically forfeits his tenure

22. Insolent and contemptuous behavior to a judge during a court of record proceeding is punishable as

    A. civil contempt
    B. criminal contempt
    C. disorderly conduct
    D. a disorderly person

23. Offering a bribe to a court clerk would not constitute a crime UNLESS the

    A. court clerk accepted the bribe
    B. bribe consisted of money
    C. bribe was given with intent to influence the court clerk in his official functions
    D. court was actually in session

24. A defendant comes to trial in the same court in which he had previously been defendant in a similar case.
   The court officer should

   A. tell him, *Knew we'd be seeing you again*
   B. tell newspaper reporters what he knows of the previous action
   C. treat him the same as he would any other defendant
   D. warn the judge that the man had previously been a defendant

25. Suppose in conversation with you, an attorney strongly criticizes a ruling of the judge and you believe the attorney to be correct.
   You should

   A. assure him you feel the same way
   B. tell him the judge knows the law
   C. tell him to ask for an exception
   D. refuse to discuss the matter

26. Assume that you are a court officer. A woman sees you in the hall and attempts to register a complaint that her husband raped her two hours earlier.
   Which one of the following is the MOST appropriate action for you to take FIRST in this case?

   A. Refer her to Family Court.
   B. Advise her that her husband has not committed any crime.
   C. Ask her for additional information about the circumstances surrounding her allegation so that you may refer her to the proper office or agency.
   D. Have her sign a criminal information in the court.

27. Which one of the following is the BEST example of a privileged communication which is NOT admissible as evidence in a court of law without the consent of the communicator?

   A. Client to his accountant
   B. Informant to a law enforcement officer
   C. Parent to his child
   D. Defendant to his spouse

28. A court officer has many contacts with the public. In these contacts, it is MOST important that he

   A. be brief and complete in his answers
   B. be courteous and helpful
   C. go along with what they ask
   D. know the law

29. Suppose a witness becomes engaged in a very heated argument with an attorney who is cross-examining him. The court officer should

   A. ask the attorney to avoid exciting the witness
   B. ask the judge if he wishes any action to be taken
   C. await the judge's order before interceding
   D. caution the witness to be more respectful

30. Suppose that you are a court officer stationed at the door of the courtroom to prevent anyone from entering while the judge is charging the jury. A man whom you recognize as a City Councilman, accompanied by a woman, attempts to enter the courtroom.
The BEST action for you to take is to

    A. apologize and explain why they cannot be permitted to enter
    B. permit the man to enter since he is a Councilman but exclude the woman
    C. permit them to enter since the judge would surely make an exception for them
    D. send a note in to the judge to find if they may be permitted to enter

31. It is desirable that a court officer acquire a knowledge of the procedures of the court to which he is assigned MAINLY because such knowledge will help him

    A. become familiar with anti-social behavior
    B. discharge his duties properly
    C. gain insight into causes of crime
    D. in any personal legal proceeding

32. Since he is a city employee, a court officer who refuses to waive immunity from prosecution when called on to testify in court automatically terminates his employment. From this statement ONLY, it may be BEST inferred that

    A. a court officer is a city employee
    B. all city employees are court officers
    C. city employees may be fired only for malfeasance
    D. court attendants who waive immunity may not be prosecuted

33. Referees of the Civil Court are former judges of this court who have served at least ten years and whose term of office terminated at the age of 55 or over, or any judge who has served in a court of record and has retired.
According to this statement, a person can be a referee of the Civil Court ONLY if he

    A. has been a judge
    B. has retired
    C. has served at least 10 years in the court
    D. meets certain age requirements

34. Assume that you are assigned to a jury room where you are to guard the jury until 4 P.M. Your relief does not arrive and the jury is still deliberating.
Of the following, the BEST action for you to take is to

    A. ask the foreman of the jury to assume responsibility until your relief arrives
    B. find out what the jurors may need, get it, and then lock them in for the night
    C. inform your supervisor but remain on duty until you are relieved
    D. wait until 5 P.M., your usual closing time, and then leave if the relief has not arrived by then

35. When, at a trial, a piece of evidence is tagged as *Exhibit A,* the CHIEF purpose is to

    A. assure its return to the owner
    B. make it possible to examine it for fingerprints without chance of error
    C. make it possible to identify and refer to it easily
    D. prevent the defendant from denying he had it

36. In one case, a mistrial was declared because the indictment used the pronoun he instead of she.
The MOST useful information a court attendant can derive from this statement is that

    A. accuracy is important
    B. mistrial is a legal term
    C. one must always use good grammar
    D. to misrepresent is criminal

37. Suppose a newspaper reporter asks you for information about what happened at a trial where the judge had ordered the courtroom cleared of reporters and spectators.
You should

    A. give him the information he wants
    B. refer him to the judge for information
    C. refuse to talk to him unless reporters from other papers are present
    D. give him misleading information

38. Assume that you are the court officer on duty outside the judge's chambers in the court house. One day, one of the judges informs you that he will be too busy that day to see any visitors, and he tells you to refer them to his secretary for new appointments. Later in the day, an important visitor comes in and asks to see the judge about urgent business.
Of the following, the BEST course of action for you to take in this situation is to

    A. ask the visitor to come back another day when the judge may be able to see him
    B. call the judge on the phone and tell him that the visitor has urgent business to discuss with him
    C. refer the visitor to one of the other judges who may be present in chambers
    D. tell the visitor that the judge is not available, but his secretary may be able to help him or make a new appointment

39. To gain a verdict against X in a trial, it was necessary to show that he could have been at Y Street at 5 P.M.
It was proven that he was seen at Z Street at 4:45 P.M. The question that MUST be answered to show whether the verdict should be against X is:

    A. How long does it take to get from Z Street to Y Street?
    B. In what sort of neighborhood is Y Street located?
    C. Was X acting suspiciously on the day in question?
    D. Who was with X when he was seen at Z Street at 4:45 P.M.?

40. If, at the instructions of the judge, a court officer calls the name of a defendant in a lawsuit and the person does not answer, the court officer should FIRST

    A. ask the judge if he called the person's name correctly
    B. call the person's name again
    C. look outside the doors of the courtroom for the defendant
    D. tell the judge the person doesn't answer

41. When X is accused of having cheated Y of a sum of money and Y is proven to have been deprived of the money, there is an additional requirement for a verdict against X.
The additional requirement is to prove that

    A. the money was stolen from Y
    B. X had the money after Y had it
    C. X had the money before Y had it
    D. X cheated Y of the money

42. Assume that you are on duty in a courtroom and during the judge's absence one of the witnesses for a pending case becomes very angry about the delay.
Of the following, the BEST action for you to take is to

   A. listen to him until he calms down and then explain the reason for the delay
   B. tell him your court is no different from any other court
   C. walk away from him so that you will not get involved in a dispute
   D. warn him that the judge may be back at any minute and will hold him in contempt

43. Assume that you are assigned to the post outside judge's chambers in the court house. A visitor tells you he has an appointment with Judge Jones who is expected to arrive shortly. He asks for permission to wait in the judge's office which is unoccupied at the present time.
For you to permit him to wait there would be

   A. *wise;* the judge would no doubt wish to speak to the man privately
   B. *wise;* it would keep the anteroom where you are stationed clear, allowing other employees to work without any disturbance
   C. *unwise;* it is rude to allow a visitor to sit alone in an office
   D. *unwise;* there may be confidential material on the judge's desk or bookcases

44. A court officer shall not receive a gift from any defendant or other person on the defendant's behalf.
The BEST explanation for this rule is that

   A. acceptance of a gift has no significance
   B. defendants cannot usually afford gifts
   C. favors may be expected in return
   D. gifts are only an expression of good will

45. When a jury is selected, the attorney for each side has a right to refuse to accept a certain number of prospective jurors without giving any reason therefor.
The reason for this is MAINLY that

   A. attorneys can exclude persons likely to be biased even though no prejudice is admitted
   B. persons who will suffer economically by being summoned for jury duty can be excused forthwith
   C. relatives of the litigants can be excused thus insuring a fair trial for each side
   D. there will be a greater number of people from which the jury can be selected

46. Where the defendant in a criminal case is too poor to afford counsel, the court will assign one and he will be paid by the government.
The principle BEST established by this statement is that

   A. it is improper for the government to provide both prosecuting and defending counsel in a trial
   B. laws are usually violated because of poverty and defendants are too poor to employ counsel
   C. only wealthy law violators may hope to be represented by competent counsel
   D. the government is obligated to shield the innocent as well as punish the guilty

47. If a visitor to the court asks foolish questions, the BEST action for the court officer to take is to

    A. answer in a brusque manner to discourage further foolish questions
    B. refer the questioner to his supervisor
    C. answer them the same way as he would any other questions
    D. ignore them since the person doesn't really expect an answer

48. A man plus a uniform makes a good court officer. This statement is FALSE because

    A. a court officer is also required to wear a badge
    B. a good court officer is not made merely by putting on a uniform
    C. it makes no mention of the fact that the uniform must be neat
    D. patrolmen as well as court officers wear uniforms

49. It is a frequent misconception that court officers can be recruited from those registers established for the recruitment of city police or firemen. While it is true that many common qualifications are found in all of these, specific standards for court work are indicated, varying with the size, geographical location, and policies of the court.
    According to this paragraph ONLY, it may BEST be inferred that

    A. a successful court officer must have some qualifications not required of a policeman or fireman
    B. qualifications which make a successful patrolman will also make a successful fireman
    C. the same qualifications are required of a court officer regardless of the court to which he is assigned
    D. the successful court officer is required to be both more intelligent and stronger than a fireman

50. One of the duties of a court officer is to assist the public with their problems.
    A PROPER exercise of this duty by a court officer would be for the officer to

    A. advise members of the public to settle their differences out of court
    B. advise a member of the public how to fill out forms required by the court
    C. lend money to a member of the public to pay the required court fees
    D. recommend a lawyer to a member of the public who does not have one

KEY (CORRECT ANSWERS)

1. A	11. C	21. C	31. B	41. D
2. C	12. C	22. B	32. A	42. A
3. D	13. D	23. C	33. A	43. D
4. C	14. D	24. C	34. C	44. C
5. A	15. A	25. D	35. C	45. A
6. C	16. A	26. C	36. A	46. D
7. C	17. D	27. D	37. B	47. C
8. B	18. C	28. B	38. D	48. B
9. B	19. B	29. C	39. A	49. A
10. B	20. B	30. A	40. B	50. B

EXAMINATION SECTION

TEST 1

DIRECTIONS: Each question or incomplete statement is followed by several suggested answers or completions. Select the one that BEST answers the question or completes the statement. *PRINT THE LETTER OF THE CORRECT ANSWER IN THE SPACE AT THE RIGHT.*

Questions 1-4 are based solely on the information in the paragraph below:

A Court Officer shall give reasonable aid to a sick or injured person. He or she shall summon an ambulance, if necessary, by telephoning the Police Department, which shall notify the hospital. He or she shall wait in a place where the arriving ambulance can see him or her, if possible, so as to direct the ambulance attendant to the patient. If the ambulance does not arrive within a half-hour, the Court Officer should call a second time, telling the department that this is a second call. However, if the injured person is conscious, the Court Officer should ask whether such person is willing to go to a hospital before calling for an ambulance.

1. The Court Officer who wishes to summon an ambulance should telephone the
    A. nearest hospital
    B. Health and Hospitals Corporation
    C. Police Department
    D. nearest police precinct

    1._____

2. If an ambulance does not arrive within half an hour, the Court Officer should
    A. ask the person injured if he/she wants to go to the hospital in a cab
    B. call the Police Department
    C. call the nearest police precinct
    D. call the nearest hospital

    2._____

3. A Court Officer who is called to help a person who has fallen on the courthouse steps and apparently has a broken leg should
    A. put the leg in traction so the doctor will have no difficulty setting it
    B. ask the person, if he/she is conscious, whether he/she wishes to go to the hospital
    C. attempt to get the story behind the injury
    D. put in a call for an ambulance at once

    3._____

4. A Court Officer who is present when a witness becomes ill while waiting to testify should
    A. wait in front of the room until the ambulance arrives
    B. send a bystander to the courtroom to page a doctor
    C. ask the witness if he/she wishes to go to a hospital
    D. call the Court Clerk for instructions

    4._____

5. "Physical and mental health are essential to the Court Officer."
   According to this statement, a peace officer must be
   A. wise as well as strong
   B. smarter than most people
   C. sound in mind and body
   D. smarter than the average criminal

6. "Teamwork is the basis of successful law enforcement."
   The factor stressed by this statement is
   A. cooperation
   B. determination
   C. initiative
   D. pride

7. "A sufficient quantity of material supplied as evidence enables the laboratory expert to determine the true nature of the substance, whereas an extremely limited specimen may be an abnormal sample containing foreign matter not indicative of the true nature of the material."
   On the basis of this statement alone, it may be concluded that a reason for giving an adequate sample of material for evidence to a laboratory expert is that
   A. a limited specimen spoils more quickly than a larger sample
   B. a small sample may not truly represent the evidence
   C. he or she cannot analyze a small sample correctly
   D. he or she must have enough material to keep a part of it untouched to show in court

8. "The Housing Authority not only faces every problem of the private developer, it must also assume responsibilities of which a private building is free. The authority must account to the community; it must conform to Federal regulations and it must overcome the prejudices of contractors, bankers and prospective tenants against public operations. These authorities are being watched for the first error of judgment or the first evidence of high costs that can be torn to bits before a congressional committee."
   On the basis of this selection, which statement would be most correct?
   A. Private builders do not have the opposition of contractors, bankers and prospective tenants
   B. Congressional committees impede the progress of public housing by petty investigations
   C. A housing authority must deal with all the difficulties encountered by the private builder
   D. Housing authorities are not more immune to errors in judgment than private developers

9. Accident proneness is a subject that deserves much more objective and competent study than it has received to date. In discussing accident proneness, it is important to differentiate between the employee who is a "repeater" and one who is truly accident-prone. It is obvious that any person assigned to work without thorough training is liable to injury until he or she does learn the "how" of it. Few workers left to their own devices develop adequate safe practices, and therefore they must be trained. Only those who fail to respond to proper training should be regarded as accident-prone. The repeater whose accident record can be explained by a correctable physical defect, correctable plant or machine hazards, or by assignment to work for which he or she is not suited because of physical deficiencies or special abilities cannot be fairly called accident-prone.

   According to the passage, people are considered accident-prone if
   - A. they have accidents regardless of the fact that they have been properly trained
   - B. they have many accidents
   - C. it is possible for them to have accidents
   - D. they work at a job where accidents are possible

9._____

Questions 10 through 12 are based on the following paragraph:

Discontent of some citizens with the practices and policies of local government leads to the creation of local civic associations. Completely outside of government, manned by a few devoted volunteers, understaffed, and with pitifully few dues-paying members, they attempt to arouse widespread public opinion on selected issues by presenting facts and ideas. The findings of these civic associations are widely trusted by the press and public, and amidst the records of rebuffs received are found more than enough achievements to justify what little their activities cost. Civic associations are politically non-partisan. Hence their vitality is drawn from true political independents who in most communities are a trifling minority. Except in a few large cities, civic associations are seldom affluent enough to maintain an office or to afford even a small paid staff.

10. The main reason for the formation of civic associations is to
    - A. provide independent candidates for local public office with an opportunity to be heard
    - B. bring about changes in the activities of local government
    - C. allow persons who are politically non-partisan to express themselves on local public issues
    - D. permit the small minority of true political independents to supply leadership for non-partisan causes

10._____

11. The statements that civic associations make on issues of general interest are
    - A. accepted by large segments of the public
    - B. taken at face value only by the few people who are true political independents
    - C. questioned as to their accuracy by most newspapers
    - D. expressed as a result of aroused widespread public opinion

11._____

12. It is most accurate to conclude that since
    A. they deal with many public issues, the cost of their efforts on each issue is small
    B. their attempts to attain their objectives often fail, little money is contributed to civic associations
    C. they spend little money in their efforts, they are ineffective when they become involved in major issues
    D. their achievements outweigh the small cost of their efforts, civic associations are considered worthwhile

12._____

13. "If you are in doubt as to whether any matter is properly mailable, you should ask the postmaster. Even though the post office has not expressly declared any matter to be nonmailable, the sender of such matter may be held fully liable for violation of law if he does actually send nonmailable matter through the mails."
Of the following, the most accurate statement made concerning this selection is
    A. nonmailable matter is not always clearly defined
    B. ignorance of what constitutes nonmailable matter relieves the sender of all responsibility
    C. though doubt may exist about the mailability of any matter, the sender is fully liable for any law violation if such matter should be nonmailable
    D. the post office is not explicit in its position on the violation of the nonmailable matter law

13._____

Questions 14 through 16 are based on the following paragraph:

What is required is a program that will protect our citizens and their property from criminal and anti-social acts, will effectively restrain and reform juvenile delinquents, and will prevent the further development of anti-social behavior. Discipline and punishment of offenders must necessarily play an important part in any such program. Serious offenders cannot be mollycoddled merely because they are under 21. Restraint and punishment necessarily follow serious anti-social acts. But punishment, if it is to be effective, must be a planned part of a more comprehensive program of treating delinquency.

14. The one goal not included among those listed in the paragraph is to
    A. stop young people from defacing public property
    B. keep homes from being broken into
    C. develop an intra-city boys baseball league
    D. change juvenile delinquents into useful citizens

14._____

15. Punishment is
    A. not satisfactory in any program dealing with juvenile delinquents
    B. the most effective means by which young vandals and hooligans can be reformed
    C. not used sufficiently when dealing with serious offenders who are under 21
    D. of value in reducing juvenile delinquency only if it is part of a complete program

15._____

16. With respect to serious offenders who are under 21 years of age, the paragraph suggests that they
    A. be mollycoddled
    B. be dealt with as part of a comprehensive program to punish mature criminals
    C. should be punished
    D. be prevented, by brute force if necessary, from performing anti-social acts

16._____

17. Statistics tell us that heart disease kills more people than any other illness, and the death rate continues to rise. People over 30 have a 50-50 chance of escaping, for heart disease is chiefly an illness of people in late middle age and advanced years. Since more people in this age group are living today than were some years ago, heart disease is able to find more victims.
    On the basis of this selection, the statement which is most nearly correct is that
    A. half the people over 30 years of age have heart disease today
    B. more people die of heart disease than of all other diseases combined
    C. older people are the chief victims of heart disease
    D. the rising birth rate has increased the possibility that the average person will die of heart disease

17._____

18. Assume that a Court Officer is allowed 25 cents a mile for the use of her automobile for the purpose of conducting defendants to and from court sessions. The first month she drove 416 miles; the second month 328 miles; the third month 2,012 miles; the fourth month 187 miles; the fifth month 713 miles; the sixth month 1,608 miles. Her expenditures for gasoline averaged $2.70 a gallon and her general average of miles per gallon was 16; she used 32 quarts of oil at $1.25 per quart and spent $351.20 on care and general upkeep of her car for the six months. Without considering the depreciation in value of her car, she would have received above her expenditures:
    A. $36.50
    B. $40
    C. $96.10
    D. $263.20

18._____

19. Assume that you borrowed $2,000 on Nov. 1, 1999, for the use of which you were required to pay simple interest semi-annually at seven percent a year. By May 1, 2005, you would have paid interest amounting to
    A. $140
    B. $280
    C. $700
    D. $770

19._____

20. A courtroom contains 72 persons, which is two-fifths of its capacity. The number of persons that the courtroom can hold is
    A. 28   B. 129   C. 180   D. 200-300

20._____

21. The total cost of 30 pencils at 18 cents a dozen, 12 paper pads at 27-1/2 cents each and eight boxes of paper clips at 5-1/4 cents a box is
    A. more than $10
    B. $1.50
    C. $4.17
    D. $1.52

21._____

22. "A" worked five days on overhauling an old car. Then "B" worked four days to finish the job. After the sale of the car, the net profit was $243. They wanted to divide the profit on the basis of time spent by each. A's share of the profit was
    A. $108
    B. $135
    C. $127
    D. $143

22._____

Questions 23-26

DIRECTIONS: Each of the following questions contains four sentences. Select the sentence in each question that is best with respect to grammar and good usage.

23. A. One of us have to make the reply before tomorrow.
    B. Making the reply before tomorrow will have to be done by one of us.
    C. One of us has to reply before tomorrow.
    D. Anyone has to reply before tomorrow.

23._____

24. A. There is several ways to organize a good report.
    B. Several ways exist in organizing a good report.
    C. To organize a good report, several ways exist.
    D. There are several ways to organize a good report.

24._____

25. A. All employees whose record of service ranged between 51 down to 40 years were retired.
    B. All employees who had served from 40 to 51 years were retired.
    C. All employees serving 40 to 51 years were retired.
    D. Those retired were employees serving 40 to 51 years.

25._____

26. A. Of all the employees, he spends the most time at the office.
    B. He spends more time at the office than that of his employees.
    C. His working hours are longer than or equal to those of other employees.
    D. He devotes as much, if not more, time to his work than the rest of the employees.

26._____

Question 27 is based on the following paragraph:

Certain inmate types are generally found in prisons. These types are called gorillas, toughs, hipsters and merchants. Gorillas deliberately use violence to intimidate fearful inmates into providing favors. Toughs are swift to explode into violence against prisoners, because of real or imagined insults. Exploitation of others is not their major goal. Hipsters are bullies who choose victims with caution in order to win acceptance among inmates by demonstrating physical bravery. Their bravery, however, is false. Merchants exploit other inmates through manipulation in sharp trading of goods stolen from prison supplies or in trickery in gambling.

27. Martins frequently beats up Smith and Brooks. Smith and Brooks provide Martins with extra cigarettes and coffee. Martins is a
    A. tough
    B. gorilla
    C. merchant
    D. hipster

27._____

Questions 28 through 30 are based on the following description of the duties of the Court Officer:

Throughout the session of the court, the officer must see that proper order and decorum are maintained in the courtroom. Above all else, silence must be constantly observed, and every possible distraction must be eliminated so as not to delay the most efficient functioning of the court.
The officer must carry out such duties as may be required by the court and clerk. Examples of such duties are directing witnesses to the witness stand and assisting the Court Clerk and counsel in the handling of exhibits. At times, the officer must act as a messenger in procuring any books from the court library that are required by the attorneys and ordered by the Court Clerk.
The enforcement of the rules of the court requires courteous behavior on the part of the Court Officer, although firmness and strictness are necessary when the occasion requires such an attitude.

28. Testimony has been given, the witnesses have been cross-examined and the attorneys have given their summations. Now the judge is charging the jury. A Court Officer has been stationed outside the courtroom door to prevent anyone from entering during the charge. The City Council President arrives, accompanied by a woman, and attempts to enter the courtroom. The Court Officer should
    A. apologize and explain why they cannot be permitted to enter
    B. permit the man to enter, since he is the City Council President, but exclude the woman
    C. permit them to enter because surely the judge would make an exception for such important people
    D. send a note to the judge to ask whether they may be permitted to enter

28._____

29. A witness who is waiting to be called to the stand appears to be very nervous. He wiggles and squirms, stands and stretches, looks over his shoulder at the courtroom door and waves to spectators. The officer should
    A. tell the witness to leave the courtroom at once
    B. handcuff the witness
    C. ask the witness to please sit still and try to restrain himself
    D. suggest to the judge that he call this witness next

30. During the course of cross-examination, a defendant frequently refers to a book that she claims has had a great influence on her life and that she claims justifies her behavior in the crime for which she is charged. In the jury box, two jurors begin a lively discussion of whether the defendant is quoting accurately. The best action for the Court Officer is to
    A. ask the Court Clerk for permission to go to the library to get the book
    B. send a messenger to get the book
    C. assure the jurors that the book is being accurately quoted and that only the interpretation is in question
    D. remind the jurors that they are not to converse in the courtroom

31. "Ideally, a correctional system should include several types of institutions to provide different degrees of custody."
    On the basis of this statement, one could most reasonably say that
    A. as the number of institutions in a correctional system increases, the efficiency of the system increases
    B. the difference in degree of custody for the inmate depends on the types of institutions in a correctional system
    C. the greater the variety of institutions, the stricter the degree of custody that can be maintained
    D. the same type of correctional institution is not desirable for the custody of all prisoners

32. "The enforced idleness of a large percentage of adult men and women in our prisons is one of the direct causes of the tensions that burst forth in riot and disorder."
    On the basis of this statement, a good reason why inmates should perform daily work of some kind is that
    A. better morale and discipline can be maintained when inmates are kept busy
    B. daily work is an effective way of punishing inmates for the crimes they have committed
    C. law-abiding citizens must work therefore labor should also be required of inmates
    D. products of inmates' labor will in part pay the cost of their maintenance

33. "With industry invading rural areas, the use of the automobile, and the speed of modern communications and transportation, the problems of neglect and delinquency are no longer peculiar to cities but are an established feature of everyday life."
This statement implies most directly that
    A. delinquents are moving from cities to rural areas
    B. delinquency and neglect are found in rural areas
    C. delinquency is not as much of a problem in rural areas as in cities
    D. rural areas now surpass cities in industry

33._____

34. "Young men from minority groups, if unable to find employment, become discouraged and hopeless because of their economic position and may finally resort to any means of supplying their wants."
The most reasonable of the following conclusions that may be drawn from this statement only is that
    A. discouragement sometimes leads to crime
    B. in general, young men from minority groups are criminals
    C. unemployment turns young men from crime
    D. young men from minority groups are seldom employed

34._____

35. "To prevent crime, we must deal with the possible criminals long before they reach the prison. Our aim should be not merely to reform the lawbreakers but to strike at the roots of crime: neglectful parents, bad companions, unsatisfactory homes, selfishness, disregard for the rights of others and bad social conditions."
The above statement recommends
    A. abolition of prisons
    B. better reformatories
    C. compulsory education
    D. general social reform

35._____

36. "There is evidence that shows that comic books which glorify the criminal and criminal acts have a distinct influence in producing young criminals."
According to this statement
    A. comic books affect the development of criminal careers
    B. comic books specialize in reporting criminal acts
    C. young criminals read comic books exclusively
    D. young criminals should not be permitted to read comic books

36._____

37. A study shows that juvenile delinquents are equal in intelligence to but three school grades behind juvenile nondelinquents. On the basis of this information only, it is most reasonable to say that
    A. a delinquent usually progresses to the educational limit set by intelligence
    B. educational achievement depends on intelligence only
    C. educational achievement is closely associated with delinquency
    D. lack of intelligence is closely associated with delinquency

37._____

38. "Prevention of crime is of greater value to the community than the punishment of crime."
   If this statement is accepted as true, greatest emphasis should be placed on
   A. execution
   B. medication
   C. imprisonment
   D. rehabilitation

39. A Court Assistant being instructed in his duties was told by the Court Clerk, "experience is the best teacher."
   The one of the following that most nearly expresses the meaning of this quotation is:
   A. A good teacher will make a hard job look easy
   B. Bad experience does more harm than good
   C. Lack of experience will make an easy job hard
   D. The best way to learn to do a thing is by doing it

40. "Once the purposes or goals of an organization have been determined, they must be communicated to subordinate levels of supervisory staff."
   On the basis of this quotation, the most accurate statement is that
   A. supervisory personnel should participate in the formulation of the goals of an organization
   B. the structure of an organization should be considered in determining the organization's goals
   C. the goals that have been established for the different levels of an organization should be reviewed regularly
   D. information about the goals of an organization should be distributed to supervisory personnel

41. "Close examination of traffic accident statistics reveals that traffic accidents are frequently the result of violations of traffic laws—and usually the violations are the result of illegal and dangerous driving behavior, rather than the result of mechanical defects or poor road conditions."
   According to this statement, the majority of dangerous traffic violations are cause by
   A. poor driving
   B. bad roads
   C. unsafe cars
   D. unwise traffic laws

11 (#1)

Questions 42 through 44 are based on the following paragraph:

The supervisor gains the respect of his staff members and increases his influence over them by controlling his temper and avoiding criticizing anyone publicly. When a mistake is made, the good supervisor will talk it over with the employee quietly and privately. The supervisor listens to the employee's story, suggests a better way to do the job, and offers help so the mistake won't happen again. Before closing the discussion, the supervisor should try to find something good to say about other aspects of the employee's work. Some praise and appreciation, along with instruction, is likely to encourage an employee to improve in those areas where he is weakest.

42. A good title that would show the meaning of this entire paragraph would be:
    A. How to Correct Employee Errors
    B. How to Praise Employees
    C. Mistakes are Preventable
    D. The Weak Employee

43. According to the preceding paragraph, the work of an employee who has made a mistake is more likely to improve if the supervisor
    A. avoids criticizing him
    B. gives him a chance to suggest a better way of doing the work
    C. listens to the employee's excuses to see if he's right
    D. praises good work at the same time he corrects the mistake

44. When a supervisor needs to correct an employee's mistake, it is important that he
    A. allow some time to go by after the mistake has been made
    B. do so when other employees are not present
    C. show his influence by his tone of voice
    D. tell other employees to avoid the same mistake

45. "Determination of total, or even partial, guilt and responsibility as viewed by law cannot be made solely on the basis of a consideration of the external factors of the case, but rather should be made mainly in the light of the individual defendant's history and development."
    The above statement reflects a philosophy of law that requires that
    A. the punishment fit the crime
    B. the individual, rather than the crime, be considered first
    C. motivations behind a crime are relatively unimportant
    D. the individual's knowledge of right and wrong be the sole determinant of guilt

46. A traffic regulation says, "No driver shall enter an intersection unless there is sufficient unobstructed space beyond the intersection to accommodate the vehicle he or she is operating, not withstanding any traffic-control signal indication to the contrary."
This regulation means that:
   A. a driver should not go through an intersection if there are no parking spaces available on the next block
   B. a driver should not enter an intersection when the traffic light is red
   C. a driver should not enter an intersection if traffic ahead is so badly backed up that he or she would not be able to go ahead and would block the intersection
   D. a driver should ignore traffic signals completely whenever there are obstructions in the road ahead

46._____

Questions 47 through 51 are based on the following passage:

A large proportion of people behind bars are not convicted criminals, but people who have been arrested and are being held until their trial in court. Experts have often pointed out that this detention system does not operate fairly. For instance, a person who can afford to pay bail usually will not get locked up.

The theory of the bail system is that the person will make sure to show up in court when he or she is supposed to; otherwise, bail will be forfeited—the person will lose the money that was put up. Sometimes a person who can show that he or she is a stable citizen with a job and a family will be released on "personal recognizance" (without bail). The result is that the well-to-do, the employed and the family men can often avoid the detention system. The people who do wind up in detention tend to be the poor, the unemployed, the single and the young.

47. People who are put behind bars
   A. are almost always dangerous criminals
   B. include many innocent people who have been arrested by mistake
   C. are often people who have been arrested but have not yet come to trial
   D. are all poor people who tend to be young and single

47._____

48. The passage says that the detention system works unfairly against people who are
   A. rich
   B. old
   C. married
   D. unemployed

48._____

49. The passage uses the expression "bail will be forfeited." Even if you had not seen the word *forfeit* before, you could figure out from the way it is used that forfeiting probably means _____ something.
   A. losing track of
   B. finding
   C. giving up
   D. avoiding

49._____

50. When someone is released on personal recognizance, this means that
    A. the judge knows that the person is innocent
    B. he or she does not have to show up for a trial
    C. he or she has a record of previous convictions
    D. he or she does not have to pay bail

51. Suppose that two men were booked on the same charge at the same time and that the same bail was set for both of them. One man was able to put up bail and was released. The second man was not able to put up bail and was held in detention. The writer of the passage would most likely feel that this result is
    A. unfair, because it does not have any relationship to guilt or innocence
    B. unfair, because the first man deserves severe punishment
    C. fair, because the first man is obviously innocent
    D. fair, because the law should be tougher on the poor people than on the rich

Questions 52 through 55 are based on the following passage:

The Court Officer has important functions in connection with control of the jury. He or she must confirm that every juror has the proper place in the box and must be constantly on watch to prevent any juror from leaving the jury box while the trial is in progress. Should a juror decide to leave the box while the case is going on, the Court Officer must first inform the judge of the juror's desire to determine whether the judge will grant or refuse the juror's wish. If the judge approves, the trial is stopped and the Court Officer is instructed to accompany the juror while he or she is out of the jury box.

In order to prevent any stoppage or mistrial, the Court Officer must not allow the juror to get out of the range of sight or hearing. The officer must always bear in mind that the juror should be returned as quickly as possible, without any unnecessary delay. The juror must not enter into any conversation with anybody or read any matter that he or she may have or that may be given by another person.

The Court Officer must be particularly careful when placed in charge of a jury that has retired to deliberate. The Court Officer must conduct the jury to the jury room and see to it that no juror talks with anyone on the way. If a juror does talk with someone, the event may afford grounds for a mistrial.

52. A juror has requested and received permission to go to the men's room. As he approaches the door, he takes out a sports magazine he has brought from home as "bathroom literature." The Court Officer should
    A. permit the juror to read the magazine
    B. check the magazine for papers that might be hidden between the pages, then let the juror read it
    C. offer the juror something of his own to read, something that he knows will not influence the juror in any way
    D. tell the juror that reading in the men's room is not permitted

53. While leading a jury from the courtroom to the jury room, a Court Officer notices a person leaning against a corridor wall making active hand motions as a juror stares intently. The *first* thing for a Court Officer to do is
    A. tell the juror to look straight ahead and keep walking
    B. step between the juror and the person so as to interrupt the juror's line of vision
    C. ask the juror what he is looking at
    D. call a police officer to arrest the person with the active hands

54. If the Court Officer ascertains that a message has been transmitted by an outside person to a juror, it would be best for the Court Officer to
    A. keep this information secret
    B. ask the juror what the message was about
    C. deliver the juror to the jury room, then discuss the matter with the Court Clerk
    D. accompany the juror to the judge and tell the judge exactly what the Court Officer observed

55. During the course of testimony, a juror begins to cough uncontrollably. The coughing is loud and distressing. The Court Officer should
    A. summon a doctor at once
    B. lead the juror from the courtroom as quickly and quietly as possible
    C. bring the juror a glass of water
    D. ask the judge what to do

KEY (CORRECT ANSWERS)

1. C	11. A	21. C	31. D	41. A	51. A
2. B	12. D	22. B	32. A	42. A	52. D
3. B	13. C	23. C	33. B	43. D	53. A
4. C	14. C	24. D	34. A	44. B	54. B
5. C	15. D	25. B	35. D	45. B	55. B
6. A	16. C	26. A	36. A	46. C	
7. B	17. C	27. B	37. C	47. C	
8. C	18. A	28. A	38. D	48. D	
9. A	19. D	29. C	39. D	49. C	
10. A	20. C	30. D	40. D	50. D	

EXAMINATION SECTION
TEST 1

DIRECTIONS: Each question or incomplete statement is followed by several suggested answers or completions. Select the one that BEST answers the question or completes the statement. *PRINT THE LETTER OF THE CORRECT ANSWER IN THE SPACE AT THE RIGHT.*

Questions 1-5.

DIRECTIONS: Questions 1 through 5 are to be answered on the basis of the following fact pattern.

A restless crowd has gathered on the lower level of the Supreme Courthouse. The judge has not yet descended from chambers and the law clerk is also missing. The forty to fifty person crowd is a mix of jurors, attorneys, and parties.

1. As an initial order of business, what should the court officer be concerned with?   1.____
   A. Taming the crowd
   B. Locating the judge
   C. Locating the law clerk
   D. Sending prospective jurors upstairs to the jury pool room

2. Two attorneys' voices have risen above all the rest. It is unclear whether   2.____
   they are shouting at one another in anger or catching up on old times. They are attracting onlookers as their conversation grows more animated.
   What is the MOST appropriate action for the court officer to take?
   A. Separate the two attorneys
   B. Ask that they lower their voices or speak privately in another area of the courthouse
   C. Sequester the jurors
   D. Ask that the two attorneys step into the courtroom to resolve their dispute

3. Some of the members of the crowd seem to be holding a single white sheet   3.____
   of paper which appears to be a summons.
   What is the MOST reasonable next step?
   The court officer should
   A. ask those a summons holders to head upstairs to check in with the clerk
   B. sequester summons holders to the side to confer with one another
   C. ask that those people sued stay put for now
   D. ask the law clerk announce herself to the possible defendants in the room

4. How should the court officer categorize and separate the crowd?   4.____
   A. Separate by the time each person arrived
   B. Separate by those with counsel present
   C. Separate by the reason he or she is at the courthouse
   D. Separate by age, gender, then race

5. In determining where each individual rightfully belongs, the court officer should be MOST familiar with which of the following?
   A. The location of each judge's chamber
   B. The times when each law clerk is scheduled to arrive at the courthouse
   C. The location of the clerk's desk, courtrooms, and preliminary hearing conference area
   D. The security desk and exits of the courtroom

5.____

Questions 6-10.

DIRECTIONS: Questions 6 through 10 are to be answered on the basis of the following fact pattern.

Jury selection has begun. Prospective jurors are gathered in the far courtroom and, after signing in, take their seats and wait to be called for sequestration.

6. During jury pool selection, two prospective jurors start to argue about a recent murder trial that made the New York Post. You should immediately
   A. shout at them to calm down or else they will be chosen for jury as punishment
   B. intervene to de-escalate the situation
   C. get the attention of the law clerk
   D. inform the judge of the jurors' behavior

6.____

7. Three women in the back of the courtroom are overhead chatting. They are being relatively quiet and not disrupting anyone around them. However, one of the women says that she knows who may be on trial today. Her nephew was arrested last night for drinking. If she is picked to serve on the jury, she says she will absolutely try to ensure he is acquitted.
You should
   A. interrupt their conversation to inform them they are being inappropriate
   B. interrupt their conversation to inform them that what they plan on doing is illegal
   C. allow them to finish their conversation in peace
   D. allow them to finish their conversation but, if selected, inform the judge of what was overheard

7.____

8. Once the jury is selected, which of the following responsibilities will MOST likely be your role?
   A. Reciting the applicable law of the case
   B. Providing the jury with opening statements
   C. Swearing in the jury
   D. Coordinating the jurors' lunch order

8.____

9. One of the jurors asks you how long the trial is scheduled to take. What is the MOST appropriate response?
   A. Trials can be extremely lengthy and take several months or take a few hours.
   B. You should pay attention to every aspect of the trial and not worry about how long you'll be here.
   C. Not respond at all as it may create bias in the courtroom.
   D. Civil trials are typically three to five days, while criminal trials are generally five to ten days.

10. After the jury is selected, one of the jurors recognizes the defendant's attorney and begins to scream at him from the jury box. You immediately start to
    A. remove the individual from the courtroom
    B. ask him to calm down and reserve his opinion about attorneys for later
    C. physically restrain the juror using force
    D. inform the judge that the juror may be biased in this matter

Questions 111-15.

DIRECTIONS: Questions 11 through 15 are to be answered on the basis of the following fact pattern.

During a civil litigation trial, multiple pieces of evidence must be presented to the jury, the witnesses, and the judge.

11. During opening statements, the plaintiff's attorney mentions that the jury will see and hear over 1,000 pieces of evidence during the trial that will convince them the plaintiff should prevail. Nearing the end of the trial, however, the plaintiff has not produced one piece of physical evidence. You should
    A. raise the issue with the judge
    B. remind the attorney during a break that they have not delivered their promise
    C. stay silent
    D. suggest the attorney produce something into evidence

12. During examination of one of the defendant's witnesses, Attorney Bob referred to a piece of evidence as the "receipt from the gas station, marked as #34." When you pick it up from the defendant, you notice the evidence is actually marked as #36. Should you intervene to correct the attorney's mistake?
    A. Absolutely not
    B. Yes, but point out to the attorney that it is marked as a different number to give him an opportunity to correct himself
    C. Yes but point out to the jury that the evidence is marked differently so that they are not confused
    D. Yes, but only to the judge in his or her chambers after the trial is complete

13. The two attorneys begin to argue with one another during the trial. 13.____
 How do you intervene?
    A. Stand between them to signal their behavior will not be tolerated
    B. Issue each of them a stern warning that they will be removed if they do not cease immediately
    C. Allow the judge to intervene first, then follow his or her instructions on how to intervene
    D. Ask the jury to remove themselves from the courtroom

14. As the two attorneys start to become more aggressive, the judge slams his 14.____
 gavel. The attorneys ignore the warning from the court.
 How would you intervene at this point?
    A. Physically restrain the plaintiff's attorney
    B. Physically restrain the defendant's attorney
    C. Stand between the two of them, hold out your arms to both sides, and order them to stop speaking directly to one another
    D. Ask the jury to remove themselves from the courtroom

15. During the trial, the defendant mutters an expletive under his breath while 15.____
 the judge gives an order as a show of blatant disrespect for the court.
 What is the MOST appropriate action to take?
    A. Allow the judge to sanction the defendant, then escort him or her out of the courtroom
    B. Physically restrain the defendant
    C. Await instruction from the judge on how to intervene
    D. Arrest the individual and remove him or her from the courtroom

16. One of the jurors appears faint and starts to wobble while seated in the jury 16.____
 box. How should you handle the situation?
    A. Let one of the jurors come to the ailing juror's aid first
    B. Alert the clerk of what you see and ask that the trial be held indefinitely
    C. Politely interject the trial proceedings and ask the juror if he or she is feeling well
    D. Quietly remove the juror from his or her seat, trying not to disrupt the trial proceedings

17. During trial, you believe that you see the defendant winking at one of the 17.____
 jurors. No one else seems to notice their interaction, including the judge and the attorneys.
 What action would you take?
    A. Alert the judge in chambers
    B. Tell the law clerk during a break in trial
    C. Interrupt the trial to make all parties aware of the behavior
    D. Confirm with the juror in question that the defendant is winking at her to determine if the feeling is mutual

18. During a sentencing hearing, the convicted defendant seems to be fiddling more than usual.
Where would you place yourself during the remainder of the hearing?
    A. As close to the judge as possible in the event you may need to protect him or her
    B. As close to the defendant's attorney as possible in the event you may need to protect him or her
    C. As close to the defendant as possible in the event you will need to restrain them
    D. At the back of the courtroom

18._____

19. In the trial of a serial killer, many prospective jurors have indicated they feel unsafe. During jury deliberations, you overhear at least two different jurors say that they want to convict the defendant simply because he has seen their faces during the trial.
What are your next steps?
    A. Interject into the jury room and inform them that their decision on that premise alone is unethical
    B. Interject into the jury room and inform them that their decision on that premise alone is unconstitutional
    C. Alert the judge immediately
    D. Instruct the jury that they do not need to look directly at the defendant in the courtroom

19._____

20. During a recess in the trial, the defendant's expert witness is seen chatting with one of the alternate jurors outside the courthouse. While it is unclear what they are talking about, it seems to be a friendly exchange of information.
What should you do before the court is called back to order?
    A. Tell the juror she must disclose her conversation with the expert witness in open court
    B. Tell the expert witness he must disclose the conversation with the juror in open court
    C. Inform the plaintiff's attorney about the conversation
    D. Inform the judge about the conversation

20._____

Questions 21-25.

DIRECTIONS: Questions 21 through 25 are to be answered on the basis of the following fact pattern.

After a TRO is issued to the plaintiff, the ex-wife of the defendant, both parties are free to go. The defendant appeared in court and rigorously opposed his ex-wife's request. His ex-wife already has sole custody of their three children, and he seems incredibly distraught by the judge's grant of her request.

21. How should you allow the parties to exit the courtroom?
    A. It is permissible and more efficient if everyone exited together.
    B. The defendant should be escorted out of the courtroom through judge's chambers.
    C. The plaintiff and her attorney should be escorted out of the courtroom first.
    D. People are free to choose how they enter and exit a building.

22. After the hearing, you see the plaintiff and the defendant's attorney chatting outside of the courtroom. Should you intervene?
    A. No, unless the conversation grows heated and someone may need to be restrained
    B. No, but you should make your presence known by moving closer to the two as they converse with one another
    C. No, because the plaintiff is not speaking directly with the defendant
    D. No

23. After the hearing, you see the defendant speaking directly with the law clerk who was present during the hearing. How should you intervene?
    A. There is no need to intervene since the hearing is over.
    B. There is no need to intervene since the law clerk is not the judge.
    C. You should inform the judge of the conversation, but not intervene in the conversation itself.
    D. You should stop the conversation immediately by announcing that it is inappropriate.

24. In a follow-up hearing, where the plaintiff is requested to extend the TRO, the defendant does not show up. Instead, the defendant's brother appears at the hearing on his behalf.
    Is the defendant's brother permitted to voice his concerns about extending the TRO?
    The defendant's brother
    A. is not a party to the action and must wait outside of the courtroom during proceedings
    B. is welcome to testify on his brother's behalf
    C. can testify on his brother's behalf as long as he remains calm while doing so
    D. can testify on his brother's behalf so long as the plaintiff's sister can testify on her behalf

25. In judge's chambers, the judge's law clerk indicates that she believes the plaintiff is lying about the defendant's alleged dangerous behavior. The judge does not agree or disagree with the clerk's statement. During proceedings, however, the clerk rolls her eyes and is not taking notes.
    The MOST appropriate step is to
    A. inform the judge after the hearing and allow the judge to handle the clerk's behavior
    B. ask that the clerk excuse herself if she cannot behave in a professional manner during hearings

C. pause the hearings and demand that the clerk leave the courtroom
D. pause the hearings and allow the clerk to correct her own behavior before the hearings can resume

KEY (CORRECT ANSWERS)

1.	A		11.	C
2.	B		12.	B
3.	A		13.	C
4.	C		14.	C
5.	C		15.	A
6.	B		16.	C
7.	D		17.	A
8.	C		18.	C
9.	D		19.	C
10.	A		20.	D

21. C
22. B
23. C
24. A
25. A

TEST 2

DIRECTIONS: Each question or incomplete statement is followed by several suggested answers or completions. Select the one that BEST answers the question or completes the statement. *PRINT THE LETTER OF THE CORRECT ANSWER IN THE SPACE AT THE RIGHT.*

Questions 1-5.

DIRECTIONS: Questions 1 through 5 are to be answered on the basis of the following fact pattern.

A trial is set to start at 9:30 A.M. At 9:45 A.M., the judge and the judge's clerk have yet to arrive. At 9:50 A.M., the law clerk enters the courtroom and takes her assigned seat beneath the judge. The judge, however, has still not appeared.

1. Should you leave the courtroom to locate the judge?   1.____
   A. Yes, but only if there is another court officer there to maintain the order of the courtroom
   B. Yes, but only if the law clerk is comfortable maintaining the order of the courtroom on her own
   C. Yes, but only if the jury has not filed into the courtroom yet
   D. No

2. At half past 10 A.M., you try to locate the judge. You see that she has entered her chambers but does not look well.   2.____
   What information do you need to ascertain your next steps?
   Whether the judge
   A. is judicially fit to hear the case
   B. is intoxicated
   C. is feeling well and needs you to adjourn the case for the day
   C. needs physical assistance by way of wheelchair or other device

3. The judge has indicated she is well enough to hear the cases for the day, but needs another few moments to collect herself. She enters her chambers and summons only one of the attorneys from the first trial.   3.____
   What is the LEAST appropriate response?
   A. Collect the attorney as requested
   B. Inform the judge that she will be commencing ex parte communications if you were to do
   C. Refuse and demand the judge recuse herself from proceedings for the day
   D. Confirm the instruction and politely inform the judge this would be inappropriate

2 (#2)

4. When you re-enter the courtroom which is still occupied with spectators, attorneys, the parties and the law clerk, who are you MOST likely to inform that the judge does not seem to be feeling well?
   A. The clerk
   B. The attorneys
   C. The entire courtroom
   D. No one

4.____

5. During the swearing-in ceremony of attorneys who passed the Bar exam, one of the attorneys stops you after going through the security check to indicate that her boyfriend is parking the car. Because she is not allowed to have her cellphone on, she cannot inform him to leave his firearm in the car. Which question would be MOST helpful in determining your next step?
   A. Does your boyfriend have a license to carry a firearm?
   B. Is the weapon loaded?
   C. Is your boyfriend dangerous?
   D. How far away is he?

5.____

6. How many alternate jurors are typically sworn in for trial?
   A. Up to 12   B. Up to 14   C. Up to 10   D. Up to 6

6.____

7. A TRO is a _____, while a QDRO is a _____.
   A. temporary restraining order; qualified domicile relations order
   B. territorial restraining order; qualified domicile relations order
   C. temporary restraining order; qualified domestic revision order
   D. temporary restraining order; qualified domestic relations order

7.____

8. There is a shortage of court officer personnel this morning, and two trials are set to start at the District Court. The first trial is a bench trial and involves a no-fault reimbursement claim. The second trial is a jury trial of a twice-convicted child rapist. Your presence is requested at both trials.
   Which should you cover?
   A. The bench trial should last a few hours, so you should cover that trial first.
   B. The jury trial has a more pressing need for law enforcement presence, so you should cover that trial in its entirety.
   C. The jury trial has a more pressing need for law enforcement presence, so you should cover the trial at least until the first recess.
   D. You are required to swear in the judge, so you must cover the bench trial.

8.____

9. The crowd of people outside the preliminary conference desk is becoming unwieldy. Attorneys are piling out of the small room in droves and seem to be overpowering the sole clerk at the front.
   What is your role in taming the crowd as it relates to the clerk?
   A. The clerk should handle the crowd, especially since they are mostly attorneys.
   B. You are responsible for calming the crowd and de-escalating any issues that arise; the clerk deserves an orderly and respectful line.
   C. You are responsible for taming the crowd by yourself and can ask for the clerk's assistance if needed.
   D. You do not need to be in or around the preliminary conference desk at all.

9.____

10. As you read the counts of the indictment, one of the jurors begins to cough uncontrollably. Should you continue reading or pause while the juror gathers herself?
You should
    A. pause and allow the juror to gather herself but not repeat the counts
    B. continue reading the indictment without pause
    C. pause and politely ask the juror if she is okay, then repeat the counts of the indictment from the beginning
    D. remove the juror

11. A twice-convicted felon is being charged with attempted rape of a minor. During a brief recess, one of the jurors returns to the courtroom to quickly grab her purse and makes eye contact with the defendant.
How do you intervene?
    A. The juror is allowed to make eye contact with the defendant, therefore no intervention is necessary.
    B. You stand in the middle of the two of them to protect the juror.
    C. You report the eye contact to the judge immediately, since bias was clearly created.
    D. You ask the judge to excuse the juror because of her impropriety.

12. Which of the following is MOST deserving of court officer intervention?
    A. A raucous crowd starting to gather a half mile outside the courthouse
    B. A disorderly jury
    C. An ex parte communication between the judge and one of the attorneys
    D. A motion hearing where one party requests an expedited trial date

13. Which of the following procedures is MOST deserving of a court officer's attention?
    A. Discovery procedures
    B. Prison handling and escort procedures
    C. Evidentiary exchange procedures
    D. Development of character witness procedures

14. One of Judge Diamond's recent decisions has sparked an outrage in the local community. Approximately one week after the decision, a peaceful and planned protest has begun outside of the courthouse.
Which of the following is MOST important during the protest?
    A. Securing the safety of Judge Diamond
    B. Controlling the media
    C. Identifying any and all aggressors in the protest
    D. Securing the safety of Judge Diamond's law clerk, Judy

15. Judge Ross is seen discussing Judge Diamond's decision with one of the media outlets covering the protest.
Which of the following actions should you be the MOST mindful of during Judge Ross's comments?
    A. Any inflammatory words against Judge Diamond
    B. The behavior of the protestors, including any persons who may charge the judge
    C. The behavior of the interviewer who may attack Judge Diamond personally
    D. The behavior of the media more generally who may try to access the courthouse while Judge Ross is speaking to the interviewer

15.____

Questions 16-18.

DIRECTIONS: Questions 16 through 18 are to be answered on the basis of the following fact pattern.

While those waiting for the court to open file into the hallway, an argument breaks out between two women and one man. When you intervene between the parties, you discover the two women are arguing over custody of a child – who is standing nearby – and the man is one of their attorneys. Barbara is the biological mother of the child. Tina raised the child from birth. Tina and her attorney, Bill, came with the child to court today.

16. Which party should stay with the child?
    A. The biological mother, Barbara, of the child should stay with the child while they await for court to begin.
    B. Tina and Bill should stay with the child since she raised the child from birth.
    C. The parties should separate and the child should come with you to a sequestered part of the courthouse.
    D. Tina and Bill should stay with the child as petitioners of the court; Barbara should wait in a separate area away from all three and refrain from contact.

16.____

17. Which of the following are Barbara and her attorney MOST likely to request in court?
    A. A No-Contact Order
    B. Order to Expunge
    C. Order to Impeach
    D. Deposition

17.____

18. Should you tell the judge about the behavior of the parties during the hearing?
    A. You can inform the judge if asked, but not during the hearing itself.
    B. You can inform the judge if asked, but should wait until the hearing is not in session.
    C. Before the hearing is set to begin, you should inform the judge of your encounter with the parties and let the judge decide how to best confront the situation between all involved.
    D. No.

18.____

19. Before the start of a trial, which is the court officer MOST likely to administer? 19.____
    Swearing in of the
       A. judge
       B. judge's clerk
       C. attorneys
       D. jury

Questions 20-25.

DIRECTIONS: Questions 20 through 25 are to be answered on the basis of the following fact pattern.

At Kings County Supreme Court, a trial of a group of alleged rapists has drawn a huge crowd of spectators at each day of the hearings. Two of the defendants are locals of Kings County while the other is a local of Bronx County. The trial date has been set and moved multiple times.

20. In determining which spectators should be allowed into the courthouse to watch the trial, which should be secured FIRST? 20.____
    A. Judge's permission
    B. Clerk's permission
    C. Jury's permission
    D. The mayor's permission

21. Which should NOT be employed in determining which spectators are allowed into the courthouse to watch the trial? 21.____
    A. The age of the spectator
    B. The spectator's affiliation with local media outlets
    C. Gender or race of the spectator
    D. The length of time the spectator has waited for the courthouse to open

22. Which of the following will the defendants MOST likely be charged with? 22.____
    A. An information
    B. A felony
    C. A misdemeanor
    D. An indictment

23. In reading the charge, which of the following is LEAST likely to appear? 23.____
    A. The name of the attorneys of record
    B. The names of the victims
    C. The number of counts of each crime
    D. The name of the judge hearing the case

24. There are likely to be multiples of which during this trial? 24.____
    A. Multiple court officers
    B. Multiple attorneys
    C. Multiple charges
    D. All of the above

25. The venue of the trial is MOST likely to be 25.____
    A. Kings County
    B. Bronx County
    C. Determined by the jury
    D. Determined by the judge

KEY (CORRECT ANSWERS)

1. D
2. C
3. A
4. D
5. A

6. D
7. D
8. B
9. B
10. C

11. A
12. B
13. B
14. A
15. C

16. D
17. A
18. C
19. D
20. A

21. C
22. B
23. B
24. D
25. D

TEST 3

DIRECTIONS: Each question or incomplete statement is followed by several suggested answers or completions. Select the one that BEST answers the question or completes the statement. *PRINT THE LETTER OF THE CORRECT ANSWER IN THE SPACE AT THE RIGHT.*

1. What is one of the MOST effective ways to disperse a large crowd in a courthouse?
   A. Start yelling that a trial is about to start
   B. Ask the crowd to form one or multiple lines
   C. Inform the crowd that they are being disruptive and should keep the volume of their voices low
   D. There aren't any effective ways to manage a crowd

   1._____

2. Which of the following is a court officer MOST likely to be volunteered for?
   A. Domestic violence awareness training
   B. Prisoner escort services
   C. Jury monitoring
   D. All of the above

   2._____

3. One of the jurors starts to strike up a conversation with you outside of the courtroom. How should you respond?
   Politely decline to
   A. engage, unless he or she is asking for directions
   B. engage, unless he or she would like to talk about the case
   C. engage, unless he or she knows you personally
   D. engage

   3._____

4. After a prisoner is escorted into the courtroom, he attempts to kick his attorney. He should
   A. be removed from the courtroom
   B. be restrained with leg restraints
   C. apologize to his attorney
   D. be forced to stand during the remainder of the proceedings

   4._____

5. A charge of attempted murder is LEAST likely to accompany a charge of
   A. murder   B. burglary   C. robbery   D. assault

   5._____

6. You begin to notice that jurors are growing sleepy and irritable towards the end of a six-week trial. Many jurors have stopped taking notes. Should you inform the law clerk or judge of their behavior?
   A. The jurors' behavior in this instance does not warrant concern.
   B. You should inform the judge's clerk so he or she can warn the jurors they may miss a critical piece of information.
   C. You should inform the judge so he or she can warn the jurors they may miss a critical piece of evidence.
   D. You should request that the jury remain alert at all times during proceedings.

   6._____

7. In an attempt to diffuse a heated argument between two attorneys at the New York County Civil Court, which factor should the court officer be MOST mindful of?
   A. The respective law firms of each attorney
   B. The volume of their voices as it carries throughout the building
   C. The likelihood these attorneys will see one another again on another case
   D. The ability for either attorney to recognize he or she is being warned about their behavior inside a court of law

7.____

8. A woman, Leslie, approaches you inside the Supreme Court and says that she has been served with a lawsuit.
Which of the following is the MOST appropriate response you can provide to Leslie?
She should have a copy of the _____ with her and refer to it, which will tell her where she would report within the courthouse.
   A. answer   B. complaint   C. summons   D. information

8.____

9. Mary produces the document, but does not know where exactly in the courthouse she should report. What is your NEXT direction?
She should
   A. check in at Courtroom A
   B. check in with the clerk's office
   C. check in at the Preliminary Conference desk
   D. wait to be called and have a seat on a nearby bench

9.____

10. Who decides whether the jurors are allowed to take notes during the trial?
    A. The judge
    B. The plaintiff's attorney, since they are bringing the case to court
    C. Jurors are always allowed to take notes during trials
    D. Jurors are never allowed to take notes during trials

10.____

11. During a trial, one of the jurors writes a question for one of the witnesses on a piece of paper and hands it to you.
What is your NEXT step?
    A. Keep it to yourself; jurors are not allowed to ask a witness questions
    B. Pass the written question to the judge, who may or may not ask the witness the question posed
    C. Decline to receive the written message
    D. Read the question to the witness on the witness stand after cross examination

11.____

12. If questions arise during the jury deliberation process, what is the role of the court officer?
    A. To deliver the written question from the jury foreperson to the judge
    B. To repeat the question orally as told to the court officer by the jury foreperson to the judge
    C. To read the written question in open court with all parties present other than the defendant
    D. To record the written question in the docket

12.____

13. In maintaining the security of the courtroom itself, what should the court officer be mindful of as it relates to non-parties to a lawsuit?
    A. Their interest level in the case
    B. How close they are sitting to the defendant and/or plaintiff
    C. Their demeanor, including a sudden change in demeanor
    D. Their note taking of court proceedings

14. A juror has informed you that she accidentally read information about the case she is serving on while she was at the supermarket last night.
    How should you respond to her?
    A. Berate her for not being more diligent in seeking out information about the case
    B. Inform the clerk that the juror should be replaced
    C. Remove the juror from the jury box and replace him or her with an alternate juror yourself
    D. Inform the judge immediately

15. The court officer is MOST likely to participate in which of the following duties?
    A. Collection of evidence at the scene of the crime
    B. Record court proceedings in the docket
    C. Schedule witnesses for trial, categorized alphabetically by their last name
    D. Assist the judge as necessary with extraneous tasks

16. One of the State's expert witnesses has failed to appear at trial when scheduled.
    Which document will the judge execute to compel his or her appearance?
    A. An indictment   B. An information
    C. An execution   D. A warrant

17. Which court proceeding takes place closest in time to an arrest?
    A. Arraignment   B. Sentencing
    C. Trial   D. Jury selection

18. Which of the following is LEAST likely to occur at the conclusion of a trial?
    A. Sentencing   B. Appeal
    C. Reversal   D. Plea bargaining

19. It has come to your attention that two of the jurors are related to one another. They are overheard talking about the case outside of the courtroom and in the court hallway.
    Should you intervene?
    A. Yes, because someone could overhear their conversation
    B. Yes, because the other jurors should be aware of how they plan on voting
    C. No, because they are siblings
    D. No, because they are outside of the courtroom and talking amongst themselves

20. How many jurors typically serve on a trial? 20.____
    A. 12 B. 18 C. 16 D. 6

21. During jury selection, the judge has already excused 25 prospective 21.____
    jurors for cause.
    How many more jurors can be excused for cause before reaching the excusal limit?
    A. 5
    B. 10
    C. The judge has reached the limit
    D. There is no excusal limit for "cause"

22. Which of the following is the jury prohibited from doing during a trial on which 22.____
    they are serving?
    A. Visiting the scene of the alleged crime
    B. Read or listen to news about the trial from outside sources
    C. Research case law that applies to the trial
    D. All of the above

23. Are court officers needed during bench trials? 23.____
    A. No, because heinous offenses are not tried by bench
    B. No, because bench trials are relatively quick
    C. Yes, because bench trials require extra security
    D. Yes, because court officers are needed for a variety of tasks during each trial

24. In New York City, jury trials are conducted at which of the following courts? 24.____
    A. Supreme Court   B. New York City Civil Court
    C. New York City Criminal Court   D. All of the above

25. A trial involving an alleged assault and battery is MOST likely to occur 25.____
    at which New York City court?
    A. Town and Village Court   B. New York City Civil Court
    C. New York City Criminal Court   D. County Court

KEY (CORRECT ANSWERS)

1.	B		11.	B
2.	D		12.	A
3.	D		13.	C
4.	A		14.	D
5.	A		15.	D
6.	A		16.	D
7.	D		17.	A
8.	C		18.	D
9.	B		19.	A
10.	A		20.	A

21. D
22. D
23. D
24. D
25. C

TEST 4

DIRECTIONS: Each question or incomplete statement is followed by several suggested answers or completions. Select the one that BEST answers the question or completes the statement. *PRINT THE LETTER OF THE CORRECT ANSWER IN THE SPACE AT THE RIGHT.*

1. One device that court officers can employ that others in the court cannot, including the clerks or judges, include
   A. power to detail
   B. use of force
   C. defensive strategy
   D. all of the above

   1.____

2. Which of the following parties is LEAST likely to be in the courtroom during every trial?
   A. Defendant
   B. Court reporter
   C. Attorneys
   D. Translator

   2.____

3. The order of the steps of a typical trial from first to last is:
   I. Opening statements
   II. Jury selection
   III. Deliberations
   IV. Oath and preliminary instructions
   The CORRECT answer is:
   A. I, II, III, IV
   B. IV, III, II, I
   C. I, II, IV, III
   D. II, IV, I, III

   3.____

Questions 4-8.

DIRECTIONS: Questions 4 through 8 are to be answered on the basis of the following fact pattern.

Pre-trial conferences are scheduled for the entire day in courtroom A with Judge Dredd presiding. Each pre-trial conference is scheduled to last 30-45 minutes.

4. During the first pre-trial conference, attorneys Bill and April become agitated with one another. Bill has accused April of ignoring the judge's order and April accuses Bill of hiding key information about the case.
   How would you diffuse the situation?
   A. The situation most likely does not require diffusing, but if they become more animated you will require they each calm down.
   B. Step between the two parties and demand respect for the court.
   C. Ask the plaintiff's attorney to step into the hallway to cool off for 5-10 minutes.
   D. Ask the defendant's attorney to step into the hallway to cool off for 5-10 minutes.

   4.____

5. During the second pre-trial hearing, the plaintiff's attorney, John, has called an expert witness to come in and testify. Your role in this process is to
   A. swear in the witness
   B. Escort the witness to the stand
   C. Record the witness testimony into the docket
   D. Relay the importance of the witnesses' testimony to him or her before they take the stand

   5.____

49

2 (#4)

6. The second pre-trial conference took longer than the time allotted. The attorneys for the third pre-trial hearing have also seemed to disappear and cannot be located.
Your NEXT step is to
   A. attempt to locate the attorneys for the hearing
   B. skip the third pre-trial hearing and hear the next conference
   C. issue a warrant for the attorneys' appearance
   D. record the lack of appearance in the docket

6.____

7. All of the following are required parties to the pre-trial hearing EXCEPT
   A. judge   B. attorneys   C. jury   D. court officer

7.____

8. The pre-trial hearing is MOST likely to take place after _____, but before _____.
   A. arraignment; jury selection
   B. deliberations; closing statements
   C. assignment; adjudication
   D. plea bargain; opening statement

8.____

9. During a court recess, you see one of the jurors walking into the judge's chambers.
You immediately
   A. halt the juror and demand he or she return to the deliberation room
   B. allow the juror to proceed, but ask the judge about the incident later
   C. allow the juror to proceed and assume they know one another personally
   D. allow the juror to proceed but inform the law clerk of the incident

9.____

10. When reading an indictment in court, each charge represents a(n)
    A. allegation of a crime   B. proven criminal act
    C. evidentiary plea   D. legal certainty

10.____

11. After a defendant has been acquitted, he or she will likely be
    A. free to leave the courthouse   B. remanded to federal prison
    C. detained until further notice   D. formally sentenced

11.____

12. Highway Patrol Officer Rowan requests to bring his firearm into the Nassau County Supreme Court as he will be testifying in a case before Judge Pirro.
Will he be able to?
    A. Yes, as he is licensed to carry the weapon
    B. Yes, as long as he provides proper identification
    C. Yes, if he is willing to discharge it in an emergency
    D. No, he must check his weapon before entering the courtroom

12.____

13. Dominic, a defense attorney, has approached you in the hallways of the New York City Civil Court. He is concerned that his client, Don, may become violent during court proceedings.
How do you handle Dominic's request to closely supervise Don while court is in session?
    A. Inform the judge of Dominic's request and allow proceedings to continue as normal
    B. Ask that another court officer be present during court proceedings

13.____

C. Request the judge to sequester the jury while Don is present
D. Ignore Dominic's request for now, until you see how Don behaves yourself

14. Jury sequestration is
    A. extremely common given the complex nature of most criminal trials
    B. becoming increasingly common
    C. more common in civil cases than in criminal trials
    D. rare

15. The judge confides in you that she believes the defendant in an ongoing trial is guilty.
    You have a duty to
    A. report the judge to the local authorities
    B. inform the clerk's office that the judge is biased
    C. there is no duty to report as the judge is free to reserve their opinion of the case
    D. there is no duty to report the judge's comment in this instance

16. It is critical after use of force to
    A. document it as well as the circumstance that provided for it
    B. recording the reactions of witnesses
    C. presenting the judge for reasoning as to why you applied it
    D. destroying any contrary evidence

17. During a witness' testimony, which may take place that will likely require your intervention?
    A. Outburst by one of the parties
    B. Disruption by the spectators in the courtroom
    C. Disagreement by the clerk and stenographer
    D. Objection by the judge

18. At arraignment, the defendant is MOST likely to
    A. state his case
    B. convince the judge of his or her innocence
    C. enter a plea
    D. gather information on his or her case from the State's attorney

19. A warrant can be issued for an individual's arrest or for
    A. search of premises outlined in the warrant itself
    B. testimony
    C. deposition of the arrested individual
    D. evidence found at the scene

20. The responsibility to record notes for the judge and listen to issues of law that may need to be researched later are reserved for the
    A. court officer   B. stenographer
    C. judge's clerk   D. jury

21. Information about the charges against the defendant, as well as the parties involved in the case, can MOST likely be found in the   21.____
    A. judge's notes B. docket
    C. information D. discovery report

Questions 22-23.

DIRECTIONS: Questions 22 and 23 are to be answered on the basis of the following fact pattern.

The clerk's office has a line out of the door, with at least eighteen people waiting to be seen. Many of the attorneys are waiting to file documents while some others are waiting for their clients.

22. How would you move the crowd out of the clerk's office?   22.____
    A. Ask that anyone who is waiting for another party to step outside
    B. Ask that anyone who is able to use the automatic filer do so
    C. Ask that only those with a question specifically for the clerk remain in the office
    D. All of the above

23. An example of a question that can only be answered by the court clerk is: 23.____
    A. When the trial is scheduled to start
    B. Where courtroom B is located
    C. The name of the attorney representing the defendant
    D. The name of the judge who hears no-fault cases

24. The opening statements in a trial are delivered by the   24.____
    A. defendant B. plaintiff C. attorneys D. judge

25. The court officer is the MOST likely party to   25.____
    A. dissolve a dispute between two jurors
    B. dissolve a dispute between the judge and the attorneys
    C. dissolve a dispute between spectators
    D. all of the above

KEY (CORRECT ANSWERS)

1. D
2. D
3. D
4. A
5. B

6. A
7. C
8. A
9. A
10. A

11. A
12. D
13. B
14. D
15. D

16. A
17. B
18. C
19. A
20. C

21. B
22. D
23. D
24. C
25. D

EXAMINATION SECTION
TEST 1

DIRECTIONS: Each question or incomplete statement is followed by several suggested answers or completions. Select the one that BEST answers the question or completes the statement. *PRINT THE LETTER OF THE CORRECT ANSWER IN THE SPACE AT THE RIGHT.*

Questions 1-5.

DIRECTIONS: Questions 1 through 5 are to be answered on the basis of the following fact pattern.

James and Sean started an accounting practice five years ago. Business quickly soured and James and Sean decided to each start their own competing business practices. While James's business flourished, Sean's practice has floundered. Sean believes James spoke poorly about him to their mutual friends, ruining his professional reputation, and went behind his back to steal clients. Sean now wants to sue James civilly.

1. How would Sean begin a civil suit against James?
   A. Sean needs to file an interpleader to compel James to court.
   B. Sean must file a motion to compel proceedings.
   C. Sean must file a complaint against James in the proper court.
   D. Sean can outline the facts of his case to the clerk who will transcribe the issues.

    1.____

2. Sean must also file a summons with the clerk.
   What is the role of the summons in initiating a lawsuit?
   A. It puts the other part on notice that a lawsuit has been filed against them.
   B. It compels discovery in a court of proper jurisdiction.
   C. It requires the other party to answer by initiating a cross-motion.
   D. It gives the other party extended time to file a counterclaim.

    2.____

3. Sean's attorney and James's attorney begin the process of exchanging information about the witnesses each side plans to call and the evidence that will be presented at trial.
   This process is called
   A. interrogation   B. discovery   C. compulsion   D. demurrer

    3.____

4. One of James' and Sean's former clients is moving to London. James' and Sean's attorneys agree to take her deposition now and use it at trial in the event she will not be able to appear.
   At trial, her testimony will be _____ and part of the record.
   A. read into evidence   B. ex parte
   C. sequestered   D. assumed credible

    4.____

5. After being notified that a lawsuit has been filed against him, James has an opportunity to answer the _____ that has been filed against him.
   A. pleadings
   B. motion to compel
   C. interpleader
   D. complaint

6. Venue refers to the district or county within a state where the
   A. lawsuit began
   B. lawsuit must be heard
   C. plaintiff resides
   D. plaintiff is domiciled

7. After both parties have agreed on a jury, the jurors are _____ by the court clerk before they are impaneled.
   A. instructed to take notes
   B. sworn in
   C. fingerprinted
   D. arranged

8. Can the prosecution compel a defendant in a criminal trial to take the stand and testify?
   A. Yes; he or she must explain what happened in open court
   B. Yes; he or she must take the stand and testify they are invoking their Fifth Amendment right against self-incrimination.
   C. Yes; he or she must take the stand but they can refuse to answer any question they choose
   D. No

9. Criminal charges are brought against a person in all of the following ways, EXCEPT
   A. citation
   B. information
   C. indictment
   D. subpoena

Questions 10-15.

DIRECTIONS: Questions 10 through 15 are to be answered on the basis of the following fact pattern.

Jason's brother, Andrew, has been arrested. Jason appears at the courthouse as soon as he hears this news. He does not know why Andrew has been arrested, but suspects it may be related to his tumultuous relationship with his ex-girlfriend who has filed a temporary restraining order against Andrew.

10. If Andrew was not arrested on a warrant, when will he be able to file a plea of guilty, not guilty, or no contest?
    A. At arraignment
    B. At trial
    C. At a preliminary conference
    D. At indictment

11. If Andrew is released from custody without a payment of money on the promise that he will appear for all hearings and for trial, the judge has released Andrew
    A. on his own recognizance
    B. with time served
    C. after a concurrent term
    D. on exculpatory evidence

12. In the alternative, if the judge sets bail for Andrew's release, he or she does so with the intent of
    A. punishing Andrew
    B. ensuring Andrew will appear for trial and al pretrial hearings for which he must be present
    C. setting a fine dependent on the type of crime alleged
    D. releasing Andrew into the custody of his responsible brother, Jason

13. Which of the following should NOT be a factor a judge may use in deciding the amount of Andrew's bail?
    A. The risk of Andrew fleeing
    B. The type of crime Andrew is alleged to have committed
    C. Andrew's age, race, and sex
    D. The safety of the community

14. During Andrew's initial appearance, the judge explains to Andrew that he has a right to a trial by jury.
    If Andrew does not want a trial by jury, what type of trial will he receive?
    A. An expedited trial   B. A bench trial
    C. A summation   D. An information

15. Andrew pleads no contest to the charges in his initial appearance.
    Andrew is effectively
    A. not admitting guilt or disputing the charge alleged
    B. admitting guilt
    C. denying the charge but admitting he will pay any fines incurred
    D. deferring his plea until a later date

Questions 16-19.

DIRECTIONS: Questions 16 through 19 are to be answered on the basis of the following fact pattern.

Jameson and Avery are neighbors. Jameson moved and purchased a home in the lot next to Avery's lot three months ago. Avery is suing Jameson for building a fence on Avery's property. Jameson attests the fence is actually being built on his own property and there is no boundary dispute. Jameson and Avery are both represented by counsel. A number of motions are filed by each party and discovery has been a lengthy process thus far.

16. Both parties serve each other requests to answer questions in writing under oath. Avery's attorney demands Jameson answer questions about the purchase of his home and dealings with the contractors building the fence. Jameson demands Avery answer questions about the property line dividing their property.
    This type of discovery is called
    A. interrogatories   B. demands
    C. summons   D. written decision

17. Avery's attorney would like to depose the property surveyor, Abe. Can Jameson and/or Jameson's attorney attend Abe's deposition?
    A. No, because Abe will be Avery's witness
    B. No, because Avery can share the information with Jameson's counsel at a later date
    C. No, because Abe's testimony may not be inadmissible in court so Jameson's presence would be futile
    D. Yes

17.____

18. Which of the following will NOT occur at the pre-trial conferenced between the parties?
    A. A deadline for discovery will be set.
    B. A trial date will be set.
    C. The judge will encourage stipulations between the parties.
    D. The judge will ask for oral arguments.

18.____

19. During discovery, both parties ascertain that Jameson built the fence on his side of the property line. Jameson's attorney asks the court to dismiss the case because there is no longer a legally sound basis to proceed.
    This request to the court is a motion to
    A. relinquish   B. dismiss   C. vacate   D. suppress

19.____

Questions 20-25.

DIRECTIONS: Questions 20 through 25 are to be answered on the basis of the following fact pattern.

A restless crowd has gathered on the lower level of the Nassau County Supreme Courthouse. The judge has not yet descended from chambers and the law clerk is also missing. The 40-50 person crowd is a mix of jurors, attorneys, and parties.

20. As an initial order of business, what should the court officer be concerned with?
    A. Taming the crowd
    B. Locating the judge
    C. Locating the law clerk
    D. Sending prospective jurors upstairs to the jury pool room

20.____

21. Two attorneys' voices have risen above all the rest. It is unclear whether they are shouting at one another in anger or catching up on old times. They are attracting onlookers as their conversation grows more animated.
    What is the MOST appropriate action for the court officer to take?
    A. Separate the two attorneys
    B. Ask that they lower their voices or speak privately in another area of the courthouse
    C. Sequester the jurors
    D. Ask that the two attorneys step into the courtroom to resolve their dispute

21.____

22. Some of the members of the crowd seem to be holding a single white sheet of paper which appears to be a summons.
What is the MOST reasonable next step?
The court officer should
    A. ask those with a summons to head upstairs to check in with the clerk
    B. sequester summons holders to the side to confer with one another
    C. ask that those people sued stay put for now
    D. ask the law clerk to announce herself to the possible defendants in the room

22.____

23. How should the court officer categorize and separate the crowd?
    A. Separate by the time each person arrived
    B. Separate by those with counsel present
    C. Separate by the reason he or she is at the courthouse
    D. Separate by age, gender, then race

23.____

24. In determining where each individual rightfully belongs, the court officer should be most familiar with which of the following?
    A. The location of each judge's chamber
    B. The times when each law clerk is scheduled to arrive at the courthouse
    C. The location of the clerk's desk, courtrooms, and preliminary hearing conference area
    D. The security desk and exits of the courthouse

24.____

25. At what juncture should the judge be notified that a large crowd has amassed outside the courtroom?
    A. Only if he or she asks
    B. After the trial has begun
    C. After the crowd has formed
    D. The clerk should be informed, but not the judge

25.____

KEY (CORRECT ANSWERS)

1.	C		11.	A
2.	A		12.	B
3.	B		13.	C
4.	A		14.	B
5.	D		15.	A
6.	B		16.	A
7.	B		17.	D
8.	D		18.	D
9.	D		19.	B
10.	A		20.	A

21.	B
22.	A
23.	C
24.	C
25.	C

TEST 2

DIRECTIONS: Each question or incomplete statement is followed by several suggested answers or completions. Select the one that BEST answers the question or completes the statement. *PRINT THE LETTER OF THE CORRECT ANSWER IN THE SPACE AT THE RIGHT.*

Questions 1-4.

DIRECTIONS: Questions 1 through 4 are to be answered on the basis of the following fact pattern.

Steven is on trial for embezzlement. The case is complex; there are eight witnesses for the prosecution and twelve witnesses for the defense, including character witnesses. Steven has filed a cross-claim against his former employer, and plaintiff, ABC Corp., Inc., for defamation of character. Steven maintains that he never stole a dime from ABC Corp., Inc. and wants ABC Corp., Inc. to issue him a public apology when the trial is over.

1. The BEST place to refer back to the testimony of one witness is 1.____
   A. the docket
   B. the judge's notes
   C. the stenographer's transcript
   D. clerk notes

2. Steven's attorney presents evidence that his client was not working on the days the theft from ABC Corp. allegedly occurred. 2.____
   What kind of evidence is Steven's counsel presenting to the court?
   A. Alibi
   B. Exculpatory
   C. Exclusionary
   D. Exemplary

3. Alexandra, a friend of Steven, testifies for the prosecution in Steven's case. Alexandra testifies that Steven told her that he embezzled money from ABC Corp. 3.____
   Steven's attorney objects to Alexandra's testimony because it is
   A. exculpatory   B. hearsay   C. untrue   D. impeachment

4. At the close of Steven's trial, oral arguments are made by _____ to the court, summarizing their position on the evidence that has been presented and their theories on the case in its entirety. 4.____
   A. jurors   B. plaintiffs   C. attorneys   D. defense

Questions 5-8.

DIRECTIONS: Questions 5 through 8 are to be answered on the basis of the following fact pattern.

April 16 is turning out to be a very busy day at the courthouse. In the morning, three cases were withdrawn by the plaintiff without a hearing, six cases were dismissed without prejudice by the judge, and two cases were settled out of court.

5. How many were decided by the judge on April 16? 5._____
   A. 0   B. 2   C. 6   D. 3

6. How many cases were heard before the judge? 6._____
   A. 3   B. 6   C. 2   D. 8

7. How many cases would the court reporter need to be present for? 7._____
   A. 6   B. 3   C. 2   D. 8

8. How many of the cases were awarded damages? 8._____
   A. 2   B. 6   C. 3   D. 0

Questions 9-12.

DIRECTIONS: Questions 9 through 12 are to be answered on the basis of the following fact pattern.

Miranda has initiated a lawsuit against her former friend, Anne, for breach of contract. Miranda referred Anne's interior design services to Miranda's boss. Anne went to Miranda's boss's house for an initial consultation and, even though Anne agreed to design three rooms in the house, she never followed through with the contract. Miranda is incredibly embarrassed by the entire situation. Anne, however, maintains that she has a reasonable excuse for not finishing the work.

9. In addition to money damages, Miranda would also like the court to compel 9._____
   Anne to execute the contract or, in other words, actually design the rooms.
   This remedy is deemed
   A. compulsion under order   B. specific performance
   C. remedy at law   D. joint and several liability

10. Miranda alleges that she suffered pain and suffering from Anne's inability to 10._____
    execute the contract.
    What type of damages are pain and suffering categorized as?
    A. Punitive   B. Special   C. Specific   D. Compensatory

11. Miranda lives in New York. Anne lives in New Jersey. Miranda's boss lives 11._____
    in Connecticut.
    When Miranda files suit in New York, the judge initially indicates that she does not have
    A. authority   B. jurisdiction   C. venue   D. domicile

12. The contract that has allegedly been breached exists between Anne and 12._____
    Miranda's boss, not Miranda. Therefore, there is no legal cause of action for
    the case to proceed. Miranda's boss is free to file the claim against Anne at a
    later date if she so chooses. The court will
    A. dismiss the action without prejudice
    B. deny the action without prejudice
    C. sustain the action
    D. abdicate as necessary

13. Nominal damages are
    A. damages awarded in name only, indicating no substantial harm was done
    B. damages to recompense the injured for the infliction of emotional distress
    C. damages to recompense the initiator of the lawsuit
    D. a reimbursement of filing fees, awarded to the person who can prove they are injured

14. The type of recovery being sought by the plaintiff is known as the
    A. order   B. punishment   C. remedy   D. issue

15. Robert approaches the clerk's desk in a panic. He says that he filed a lawsuit against his cousin, Mike, but neglected to add his cousin's friend, Rory, to the suit. What action is Robert attempting to take?
    A. Amending the complaint
    B. Adding an addendum to the summons
    C. Re-issuing a summons
    D. Redacting the answer

Questions 16-20.

DIRECTIONS: Questions 16 through 20 are to be answered on the basis of the following fact pattern.

Daniel and Patrick sue one another civilly. Daniel sues Patrick for intentional infliction of emotional distress and Patrick countersues Daniel for assault. Both causes of action stem from a physical altercation which took place at a youth hockey game where Daniel and Patrick's sons played against one another. At trial, the judge found that Daniel started the fight and attacked Patrick and found, by extension, that Patrick was not a contributor in the altercation.

Daniel appealed the decision to an appellate court. Daniel's attorney argued that the trial court erred, as a matter of law, in finding that Daniel was the sole initiator of the altercation and ignored evidence to the contrary. Appellate courts generally render decisions by a panel. The panel in Daniel's appeal was comprised of three justices. The appellate court agreed with the trial court's finding of fault.

16. The ultimate disposition of this case was the appellate court
    A. affirmed the lower court's decision
    B. remanded the lower court's decision
    C. reversed the lower court's decision
    D. acquitted Daniel of all charges

17. An opinion from the entire panel of justices is known as a
    A. per curiam decision   B. affirmative decision
    C. stare decisis   D. en banc order

18. One of the judges agrees with the decision of the court, but disagrees with the reasoning of the conclusion. The judge decides to write his own opinion. This is deemed a
    A. dissenting opinion   B. remedial decision
    C. concurring opinion   D. recurrent opinion

19. Suppose that one of the judges disagrees entirely with the ruling. How will the judgment be altered because of the disagreement? The judgment
    A. is unaffected because the majority voted in agreement with the trial court
    B. is unaffected because this judge did not author a dissenting opinion
    C. is unaffected because oral arguments were not made before the panel
    D. will be overturned

20. The appellate court still requires _____, even if it is established by the trial court, known as original _____.
    A. domicile; venue
    B. venue; jurisdiction
    C. jurisdiction; jurisdiction
    D. jurisdiction; domicile

21. The legal theory upon which a case is based is called a
    A. basis
    B. decisis
    C. cause of action
    D. precedent

Questions 22-25.

DIRECTIONS: Questions 22 through 25 are to be answered on the basis of the following fact pattern.

Last July, Sarah stole Alexis's car and took it for a joyride along Main Street. After a long joyride, Sarah decided to pick up Ashley at Ashley's apartment. Although Ashley asked when Sarah bought a new car, Sarah lied and told Ashley that it was her aunt's car that she borrowed with permission. Sarah and Ashley went on another joyride, this time driving up to 90 miles per hour on the highways around town. After three hours, Ashley asked to go home and Sarah obliged. After Sarah dropped Ashley back off at her apartment, Sarah sped through a busy intersection and crashed the car. The car was totaled.
Alexis has filed a lawsuit against both Sarah and Ashley.

22. Alexis is determined to sue both Sarah and Ashley for conversion, or the wrongful act of dominion or control over another person's property. However, after meeting with her attorney, Alexis decided she may not be able to prove each _____ of the alleged crime against Ashley.
    A. stage
    B. element
    C. circumstance
    D. remedy

23. After Alexis initiated her lawsuit against Sarah and Ashley, Ashley requested the court to remove her from the lawsuit altogether. She attested that she could not have participated in a crime if she did not know the car was stolen. Her request to the court will come in the form of a
    A. notice   b. motion   C. termination   D. demand

24. Ashley's attorney asks the judge to instruct the jury that it can consider mitigating factors in rendering a verdict against Ashley.
An example of a mitigating factor in this scenario would MOST likely be:
   A. Ashley does not know Alexis
   B. Sarah is no longer friends with Alexis
   C. Ashley asked Sarah about the origins of the car and Sarah's reply was untruthful
   D. Ashley and Sarah were working in cahoots to steal Alexis's car

25. During the time of the crime, Sarah was a minor. A minor is legally defined as
   A. someone who cannot think for themselves
   B. anyone under 21
   C. a legally emancipated individual
   D. an infant or individual under the age of legal competence

KEY (CORRECT ANSWERS)

1.	C		11.	B
2.	B		12.	A
3.	B		13.	A
4.	C		14.	C
5.	C		15.	A
6.	B		16.	A
7.	A		17.	A
8.	D		18.	C
9.	B		19.	A
10.	D		20.	C

21. C
22. B
23. B
24. C
25. D

TEST 3

DIRECTIONS: Each question or incomplete statement is followed by several suggested answers or completions. Select the one that BEST answers the question or completes the statement. *PRINT THE LETTER OF THE CORRECT ANSWER IN THE SPACE AT THE RIGHT.*

Questions 1-4.

DIRECTIONS: Questions 1 through 4 are to be answered on the basis of the following fact pattern.

A complex civil litigation suit is set to begin between ABC Insurance Corp. and DEF Indemnity Corp. Adam represents ABC Insurance and Jane represents DEF Indemnity Corp. Multiple extensions have been granted to either side to conduct more extensive discovery. At the last conference scheduled before trial, the presiding judge is notably frustrated at the requested delays from both Adam and Jane. The presiding judge would like both parties to stipulate to as many points as possible.

1. Adam and Jane appear in the permanent record as _____ unless either withdrawn or are otherwise removed from the case.
    A. attorneys in time
    B. attorneys of record
    C. attorneys of the case
    D. permanent attorneys

2. The judge asks whether the parties have attempted to settle this matter in another forum, such as binding
    A. decision-making
    B. arbitration
    C. neutral court
    D. judgment arena

3. While the judge would like the parties to settle, he quickly realizes that it is not a possibility between these two parties. Adam and Jane continue to argue about various issues, including expert witnesses. Adam argues that Jane's expert witness, who will testify about financial crimes, is a quack. In response, Jane offers that her witness be _____, or testify under oath at a date prior to trial.
    A. sworn in   B. indemnified   C. deposed   D. saddled

4. Which of the following is the LEAST appropriate behavior of the judge during a pretrial conference?
    A. Providing advice on Adam and Jane's legal strategy for trial
    B. Asking the parties to stipulate to the facts
    C. Remaining indifferent about the witnesses each party plans to call at trial
    D. Setting a date for trial more than three months away

5. A lawsuit with a single cause of action being breach of contract will be classified as what type of suit?
    A. Criminal   B. Divisional   C. Situational   D. Civil

6. Sheila's mother passed away last week. She comes to the courthouse and asks about the probate process. You inform her that probate may not be necessary if she is the person named in the will as the individual who will administer her mother's estate.
   This individual is otherwise known as the
   A. administrator B. guarantor C. creditor D. executor

7. Brandy would like her juvenile record expunged. What is she seeking to do? She is requesting
   A. her record, or a portion of her record, be removed
   B. her record be sealed
   C. her record be unsealed
   D. to make her record unavailable to creditors

8. Having never met Jamie, a pro se litigant, Judge Smith strikes up a friendly conversation about the recent political climate in the elevator with him on the way to the courtroom. In the courtroom that afternoon, Jamie enters his appearance and says, "You and I are clearly already on the same page, Judge" in open court. Jamie's adversary, Courtney, requests that the judge recuse himself from the case. Why?
   A. Jamie and Judge Smith's political affiliations are unsavory.
   B. Judge Smith is clearly biased as evidenced by Jamie's comment.
   C. Judge Smith and Jamie have partaken in en banc communications.
   D. Judicial disqualification is appropriate if a conflict of interest would affect a judge's ruling

9. Emily appears at court with a crumbled notice in her hands. The clerk asks that you speak with Emily directly because Emily
   A. may be in danger of hurting others or herself
   B. may have a legal question that needs answering
   C. is in default and may need to be arrested
   D. would like to apply for a job at the courthouse

10. A conditional release from incarceration is known as
    A. an expungement   B. a restitution
    C. parole   D. reduced sentence

11. Tom paid a contractor to cut down a large pine tree in front of his house. The tree had grown so tall that it has started to interfere with the power lines running parallel to the street. As the contractor cut down the tree, a large gust of wind blew and the tree crashed down on top of his neighbor, Dane's, roof. Dane is suing Tom for failure to exercise the degree of care that a reasonable person would have exercised in the same circumstance.
    Dane is suing Tom for
    A. lack of judgment   B. breach of contract
    C. negligence   D. conversion

12. Lawyers are generally prohibited from asking _____ questions of their own witnesses because they are suggestive, or prompt the witness to answer in a certain way.
    A. leading   B. direct   C. cross   D. sustainable

13. One process that is generally private, and not heard in open court is(are)
    A. testimony of expert witnesses
    B. swearing in of jurors
    C. objections
    D. plea bargaining

14. The burden of proof in a civil case is _____ stringent than that in a criminal case.
    A. less   B. more   C. equally   D. substantially

15. Justin is an attorney for Samuel. During Justin's closing arguments, he states that Samuel is innocent and would never harm another living being. May jurors consider Justin's statement made during closing arguments as evidence or fact?
    A. Yes, but only if compelling
    B. Yes, but only under the circumstances explained by the judge
    C. Yes, unconditionally
    D. No

16. In reviewing the court transcript, which of the following is the attorney LEAST likely to find?
    A. The judge's opinion on the case
    B. Testimony of the petitioner
    C. Attorneys of record
    D. Names of the expert witnesses

17. A mandatory injunction has the effect of
    A. requiring a party to do a particular act
    B. providing the option of a party to do a particular act
    C. requiring a party to report their actions
    D. providing the party an option to report their actions

18. James approaches the clerk's desk and asks how, generally, judges make their decisions on legal matters.
    The MOST correct answer would be based on
    A. case law, or the body of all court decisions which govern or provide precedent on the same legal issue before the judge
    B. case law, personal opinion and oral arguments by attorneys
    C. case law, oral arguments by attorneys and the defendant's rap sheet
    D. "stare decisis" or that which has already been decided

19. Which of the following individuals is LEAST likely to serve on a jury?
    A. Susan, who has been called numerous times but never served on a jury
    B. Bill, a supporter of labor unions and freelance political columnist
    C. Gary, who served on a murder trial 10 years ago
    D. Amy, a 16-year-old genius who just finished her junior year of college

20. If a grand jury decides there is enough evidence to move forward with criminal charges against a group or individual, they return a(n)
    A. information B. indictment C. warrant D. seizure

21. Which of the following is MOST likely to cause an outburst in a courtroom?
    A. Reading of the jury instructions
    B. Sequestration of the jury
    C. Reading of the sentence
    D. Plea deal proceedings

22. During a lengthy murder trial, it is discovered that two of the jurors have been romantically involved. They have conspired with one another to enter votes of "not guilty" and attempt to sway other jurors in their favor in an attempt to close out deliberations early.
    What is the likely outcome of the trial?
    A. Hung jury
    B. Mistrial
    C. Acquittal
    D. Defensive charge

23. The judge's charge to the jury is also known as
    A. voir dire
    B. en banc
    C. jury instructions
    D. sua sponte

24. Who is MOST likely to deliver the sentence to the convicted?
    A. Bailiff
    B. Jury
    C. Judge
    D. Jury foreperson

25. A motion for directed verdict is made
    A. without the jury present
    B. with only the jury foreperson present
    C. with the entire jury present
    D. with only the alternate jurors present

KEY (CORRECT ANSWERS)

1.	B		11.	C
2.	B		12.	A
3.	C		13.	D
4.	A		14.	A
5.	D		15.	D
6.	D		16.	A
7.	A		17.	A
8.	D		18.	A
9.	A		19.	D
10.	C		20.	B

21. C
22. B
23. C
24. C
25. A

TEST 4

DIRECTIONS: Each question or incomplete statement is followed by several suggested answers or completions. Select the one that BEST answers the question or completes the statement. *PRINT THE LETTER OF THE CORRECT ANSWER IN THE SPACE AT THE RIGHT.*

Questions 1-6.

DIRECTIONS: Questions 1 through 6 are to be answered on the basis of the following fact pattern.

Damien is accused of heinous crimes against a minor. He is charged with rape of a child, conspiracy to murder, and armed robbery. During the commission of the crime, it is alleged that Damien called his friend, Alex, and asked that he come to the scene of the crime and kill the minor's parents. Damien and Alex are on trial together, but Alex is charged with lesser crimes given that his involvement may have been limited. The trial is lengthy and a large crowd has gathered outside the courtroom each day of testimony.

1. The prosecutors allege that Alex agreed to help Damien commit the crimes because Damien has a propensity for violence and may have threatened to kill Alex if he did not help. The prosecutors are presenting
    A. evidence   B. testimony   C. motive   D. supposition

    1._____

2. The intense nature of the court proceedings may require which of the following?
    A. Increased law enforcement presence
    B. Increased legal analysis
    C. More jurors
    D. More law clerks

    2._____

3. During the presentation of evidence, the judge is likely to require exhibits be passed to the court officer, who will then present them to the jury, instead of the attorneys, to ensure
    A. the evidence is not tampered with by the attorneys
    B. a smooth and orderly presentation
    C. the materials are not lost in transit
    D. each item in evidence is numbered correctly

    3._____

4. Evidence against Damien is presented first. The prosecutor presents testimony from eyewitnesses, other than Alex, that place Damien at the scene of the crime.
    This evidence is deemed
    A. inculpatory   B. explanatory   C. involuntary   D. dismissive

    4._____

5. Alex decides to take the stand in his own defense. While on the stand, he declines to invoke his right not to incriminate himself.
Alex is referring to which Constitutional Amendment?
   A. Eighth   B. Ninth   C. Fourth   D. Fifth

6. During the presentation of closing arguments, the victims' stepfather, Bob, becomes enraged. As the defense attorney speaks to the jury, Bob starts screaming and demands justice.
The MOST appropriate response to Bob's disruption of court proceedings is to
   A. let Bob calm down on his own
   B. eject Bob from the courtroom
   C. handcuff Bob
   D. allow Bob to continue after a stern warning that he lower his voice

7. During downtime, which of the following is the LEAST appropriate action a court officer can take?
   A. Monitoring courtrooms and hallways for suspicious activity
   B. Managing the metal detectors
   C. Watching and managing doorways
   D. Answering legal questions from the general public

8. Jessica approaches one of the court officers in the entrance of the Herkimer County Supreme Court and states that she has a disassembled firearm in her vehicle.
The MOST appropriate response to this information is:
   A. Make other court officers aware of her admission and monitor Jessica's comings and goings
   B. Detain Jessica until police officers arrive
   C. Arrange for Jessica to bring the firearm into the courthouse so that it can be locked away in a storage locker
   D. Ask Jessica for her license to carry and make a photocopy for court records

9. Which of the following is MOST likely to occur after opening arguments in a trial?
   A. Presentation of evidence   B. Jury instructions
   C. Closing arguments   D. Arraignment

10. After the judge orders Paul to stay away from Amy in a ruling regarding Amy's request for a temporary restraining order, Paul is overheard in a court hallway that he plans on killing Amy and the judge.
The first party that should be notified is
   A. the law clerk   B. local police department
   C. the jurors in Amy and Paul's trial   D. the U.S. Marshals

Questions 11-15.

DIRECTIONS: Questions 11 through 15 are to be answered on the basis of the following fact pattern.

During a highly publicized and complex trial in the Oswego County Supreme Court, jurors have been isolated from friends and family members. The jurors are staying at the local Ramada Inn. Multiple court officers have been dispatched to the hotel and oversee the transport of the jurors to the courtroom each morning and night.

11. The jurors are being
    A. sequestered   B. influenced   C. disposed   D. indicted

12. One of the jurors has fallen ill during the trial. Given that one juror can no longer serve, what is the procedure?
    A. The jury will be comprised of eleven jurors.
    B. The trial will halt until the ill juror feels better.
    C. An alternate juror will serve on the jury.
    D. The jury will go on with six jurors.

13. One of the jurors has been seen texting on his cellphone during the transport to the hotel at night.
    Which is the LEAST appropriate response to this rumor?
    A. Confiscate the juror's phone and inform the judge
    B. Ask to see the juror's text messages so you can delete the text history
    C. Ignore the rumors
    D. Tell the other court officer about the rumor but otherwise ignore it

14. What is the likely outcome of the texting juror?
    The juror will
    A. likely be allowed to remain on the jury
    B. likely be asked to hand over his or her phone and other electronic devices
    C. likely be dismissed form the trial and replaced
    D. be allowed to keep communicating with the outside but will be closely monitored

15. The trial has finally ended and the jury has started deliberations. After nearly two weeks, the jury has been unable to arrive at a decision.
    This is deemed a
    A. final jury   B. deliberate jury
    C. mistrial   D. hung jury

16. A previously convicted felon, Tim, is on trial for the conspiracy to kill his cellmate in prison. Tim is MOST likely going to be _____ at all times during court proceedings.
    A. restrained   B. redacted
    C. unaccompanied   D. redeemed

17. Which of the following is a court officer duty that specifically relates to witness testimony?
    A. Assisting witnesses leaving the stand
    B. Help witnesses remember their testimony
    C. Relay messages directly from the witnesses to the judge
    D. Engage witnesses in the service of the domestic violence unit if needed

17.____

18. As Sarah waits for the judge to enter the courtroom and commence hearings, she opens her purse and pulls out a sandwich and begins to eat it. The court officer informs her that she cannot eat in the courtroom and must leave the building if she want to have food or a beverage. Sarah continues to eat the food and laments that since the judge is not in the courtroom, she should be able to eat.
    The court officer is MOST likely going to
    A. eject Sarah from the courtroom
    B. allow Sarah to eat until the judge enters the courtroom
    C. allow Sarah to eat as she has a valid point
    D. confiscate Sarah's sandwich

18.____

19. Which of the following may require the law clerk's assistance?
    A. Removal of an unruly individual from the courtroom
    B. Determining which person in a court proceeding is the plaintiff, defendant, or witness
    C. Obtaining personal information from the defendant
    D. Relaying a message to the judge that relates to a personal matter

19.____

Questions 20-25.

DIRECTIONS: Questions 20 through 2 are to be answered on the basis of the following fact pattern.

Eric's attorney, Rich, alleges that Eric is not ___1___ to stand trial. As a child, Eric was the victim of abuse and as a result may be mentally ill. Eric is accused of murder in the second degree. At trial, Eric's friend, Ross, claims that Eric told him he murdered a young woman. Rich objects to Ross's testimony as it is ___2___ and not conclusory of Eric's guilt. Another witness claims that they saw Eric at the scene of the crime, but does not remember seeing Eric with another person. This witness is a twice-convicted felon and is not deemed ___3___ by the jury. At the conclusion of the evidence as presented by the attorney, Eric is found guilty.

20. Fill in blank #1:
    A. mentally well   B. competent   C. jurisdiction   D. venue

20.____

21. Fill in blank #2:
    A. motive   B. evidentiary   C. hearsay   D. realistic

21.____

22. Fill in blank #3:
    A. credible   B. justifiable   C. plausible   D. tangible

22.____

23. The victim's family is allowed to make a victim impact statement. 23.____
At which juncture is the victim impact statement allowed to be heard?
    A. Sentencing and/or subsequent parole hearings
    B. Prior to jury instructions
    C. After closing arguments
    D. As testimony read into the record

24. Closing arguments enable each party's attorney to 24.____
    A. present new evidence in the trial
    B. summarize the legal and factual points for their side of the case
    C. analyze the jury's reaction to their evidence
    D. provide additional details and analysis to the opinions of the expert witnesses

25. Sylvia asks that a court officer escort her to her car after her foreclosure 25.____
proceedings. Her foreclosure hearings were not adversarial and Sylvia does
not appear to be in imminent harm.
The MOST appropriate response to Sylvia's request is to
    A. ensure there is proper officer coverage inside the courthouse, then escort Sylvia to her car
    B. decline Sylvia's request given that she was only in the courthouse for foreclosure proceedings
    C. decline Sylvia's request as she is not in imminent danger
    D. ignore Sylvia

KEY (CORRECT ANSWERS)

1.	C		11.	A
2.	A		12.	C
3.	B		13.	C
4.	A		14.	C
5.	D		15.	D
6.	B		16.	A
7.	D		17.	A
8.	A		18.	A
9.	A		19.	B
10.	B		20.	B

21.	C
22.	A
23.	A
24.	B
25.	A

EVALUATING INFORMATION AND EVIDENCE
EXAMINATION SECTION
TEST 1

DIRECTIONS: Each question or incomplete statement is followed by several suggested answers or completions. Select the one that BEST answers the question or completes the statement. *PRINT THE LETTER OF THE CORRECT ANSWER IN THE SPACE AT THE RIGHT.*

Questions 1-9.

DIRECTIONS: Questions 1 through 9 measure your ability to (1) determine whether statements from witnesses say essentially the same thing and (2) determine the evidence needed to make it reasonably certain that a particular conclusion is true.

1. Which of the following pairs of statements say essentially the same thing in two different ways?
   I. If you get your feet wet, you will catch a cold.
      If you catch a cold, you must have gotten your feet wet.
   II. If I am nominated, I will run for office.
      I will run for office only if I am nominated.
   The CORRECT answer is:
   A. I only B. I and II C. II only D. Neither I nor II

   1.____

2. Which of the following pairs of statements say essentially the same thing in two different ways?
   I. The enzyme Rhopsin cannot be present if the bacterium Trilox is absent.
      Rhopsin and Trilox always appear together.
   II. A member of PENSA has an IQ of at least 175.
      A person with an IQ of less than 175 is not a member of PENSA
   The CORRECT answer is;
   A. I only B. I and II C. II only D. Neither I nor II

   2.____

3. Which of the following pairs of statements say essentially the same thing in two different ways?
   I. None of Finer High School's sophomores will be going to the prom.
      No student at Finer High School who is going to the prom is a sophomore.
   II. If you have 20/20 vision, you may carry a firearm.
      You may not carry a firearm unless you have 20/20 vision.
   The CORRECT answer is:
   A. I only B. I and II C. II only D. Neither I nor II

   3.____

2 (#1)

4. Which of the following pairs of statements say essentially the same thing in two different ways?
   I. If the family doesn't pay the ransom, they will never see their son again.
      It is necessary for the family to pay the ransom in order for them to see their son again.
   II. If it is raining, I am carrying an umbrella.
       If I am carrying an umbrella, it is raining.
   The CORRECT answer is:
   A. I only   B. I and II   C. II only   D. Neither I nor II

4._____

5. Summary of Evidence Collected to Date:
   In the county's maternity wards, over the past year, only one baby was born who did not share a birthday with any other baby.
   Prematurely Drawn Conclusion: At least one baby was born on the same day as another baby in the county's maternity wards.
   Which of the following pieces of evidence, if any, would make it reasonably certain that the conclusion drawn is true?
   A. More than 365 babies were born in the county's maternity wards over the past year.
   B. No pairs of twins were born over the past year in the county's maternity wards.
   C. More than one baby was born in the county's maternity wards over the past year.
   D. None of the above

5._____

6. Summary of Evidence Collected to Date:
   Every claims adjustor for MetroLife drives only a Ford sedan when on the job.
   Prematurely Drawn Conclusion: A person who works for MetroLife and drives a Ford sedan is a claims adjustor.
   Which of the following pieces of evidence, if any, would make it reasonably certain that the conclusion drawn is true?
   A. Most people who work for MetroLife are claims adjustors.
   B. Some people who work for MetroLife are not claims adjustors.
   C. Most people who work for MetroLife drive Ford sedans
   D. None of the above

6._____

7. Summary of Evidence Collected to Date:
   Mason will speak to Zisk if Zisk will speak to Ronaldson.
   Prematurely Drawn Conclusion: Jones will not speak to Zisk if Zisk will speak to Ronaldson.
   Which of the following pieces of evidence, if any, would make it reasonably certain that the conclusion drawn is true?
   A. If Zisk will speak to Mason, then Ronaldson will not speak to Jones.
   B. If Mason will speak to Zisk, then Jones will not speak to Zisk.
   C. If Ronaldson will speak to Jones, then Jones will speak to Ronaldson.
   D. None of the above

7._____

78

8. **Summary of Evidence Collected to Date**:
   No blue lights on the machine are indicators for the belt drive status.
   Prematurely Drawn Conclusion: Some of the lights on the lower panel are not indicators for the belt drive status.
   Which of the following pieces of evidence, if any, would make it reasonably certain that the conclusion drawn is true?
   A. No lights on the machine's lower panel are blue.
   B. An indicator light for the machine's belt drive status is either green or red.
   C. Some lights on the machine's lower panel are blue.
   D. None of the above

8._____

9. **Summary of Evidence Collected to Date**:
   Of the four Sweeney sisters, two are married, three have brown eyes, and three are doctors.
   Prematurely Drawn Conclusion: Two of the Sweeney sisters are brown-eyed, married doctors.
   Which of the following pieces of evidence, if any, would make it reasonably certain that the conclusion is true?
   A. The sister who does not have brown eyes is married.
   B. The sister who does not have brown eyes is not a doctor, and one who is not married is not a doctor.
   C. Every Sweeney sister with brown eyes is a doctor.
   D. None of the above

9._____

Questions 10-14.

DIRECTIONS: Questions 10 through 14 refer to Map #5 and measure your ability to orient yourself within a given section of town, neighborhood or particular area. Each of the questions describes a starting point and a destination. Assume that you are driving a car in the area shown on the map accompanying the questions. Use the map as a basis for the shortest way to get from one point to another without breaking the law.

On the map, a street marked by arrows, or by arrows and the words "One Way," indicates one-way travel and should be assumed to be one-way for the entire length, even when there are breaks or jogs in the street. EXCEPTION: A street that does not have the same name over the full length.

4 (#1)

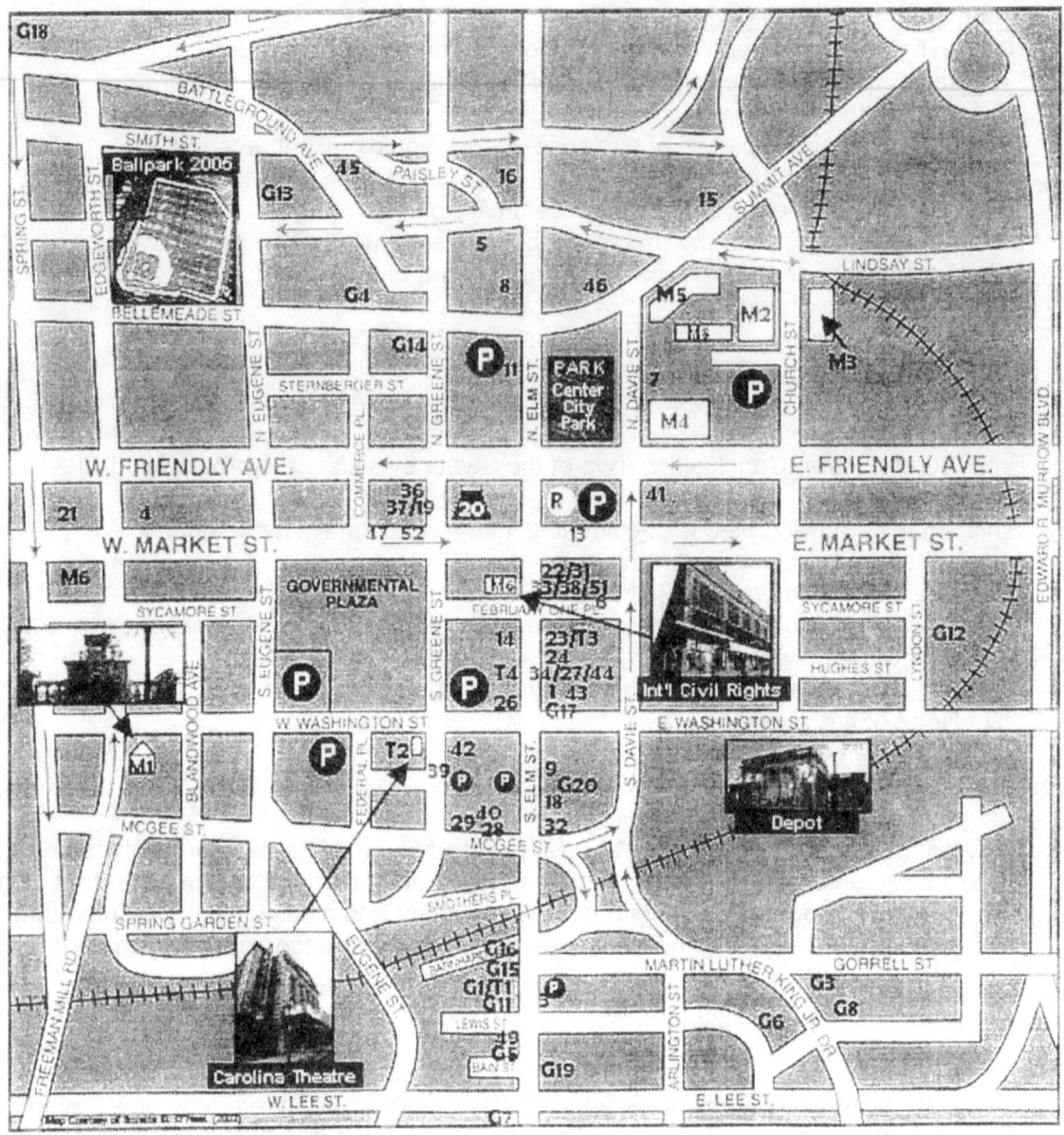

Map #5

10. The SHORTEST legal way from the depot to Center City Park is   10.____
    A. north on Church, west on Market, north on Elm
    B. east on Washington, north on Edward R. Murrow Blvd., west on Friendly Ave.
    C. west on Washington, north on Greene, east on Market, north on Davie
    D. north on Church, west on Friendly Ave.

11. The SHORTEST legal way from the Governmental Plaza to the Ballpark is   11.____
    A. west on Market, north on Edgeworth
    B. west on Market, north on Eugene
    C. north on Greene, west on Lindsay
    D. north on Commerce Place, west on Bellemeade

12. The SHORTEST legal way from the International Civil Rights Building to the   12.____
    building marked "M3" on the map is
    A. east on February One Place, north on Davie, east on Friendly Ave., north
       on Church
    B. south on Elm, west on Washington, north on Greene, east on Market,
       north on Church
    C. north on Elm, east on Market, north on Church
    D. north on Elm, east on Lindsay, south on Church

13. The SHORTEST legal way from the Ballpark to the Carolina Theatre is   13.____
    A. east on Lindsay, south on Greene
    B. south on Edgeworth, east on Friendly Ave., south on Greene
    C. east on Bellemeade, south on Elm, west on Washington

14. A car traveling north or south on Church Street may NOT go   14.____
    A. west onto Friendly Ave.   B. west onto Lindsay
    C. east onto Market   D. west onto Smith

Questions 15-19.

DIRECTIONS: Questions 15 through 19 refer to Figure #3, on the following page, and
              measure your ability to understand written descriptions of events. Each
              question presents a description of an accident or event and asks you which of
              the following five drawings in Figure #3 BEST represents it.
              In the drawings, the following symbols are used:
              Moving vehicle ⌂   Non-moving vehicle ⌂
              Pedestrian or bicyclist •
              The path and direction of travel of a vehicle or pedestrian is indicated by a solid
              line.
              The path and direction of travel of each vehicle or pedestrian directly involved
              in a collision from the point of impact is indicated by a dotted line.

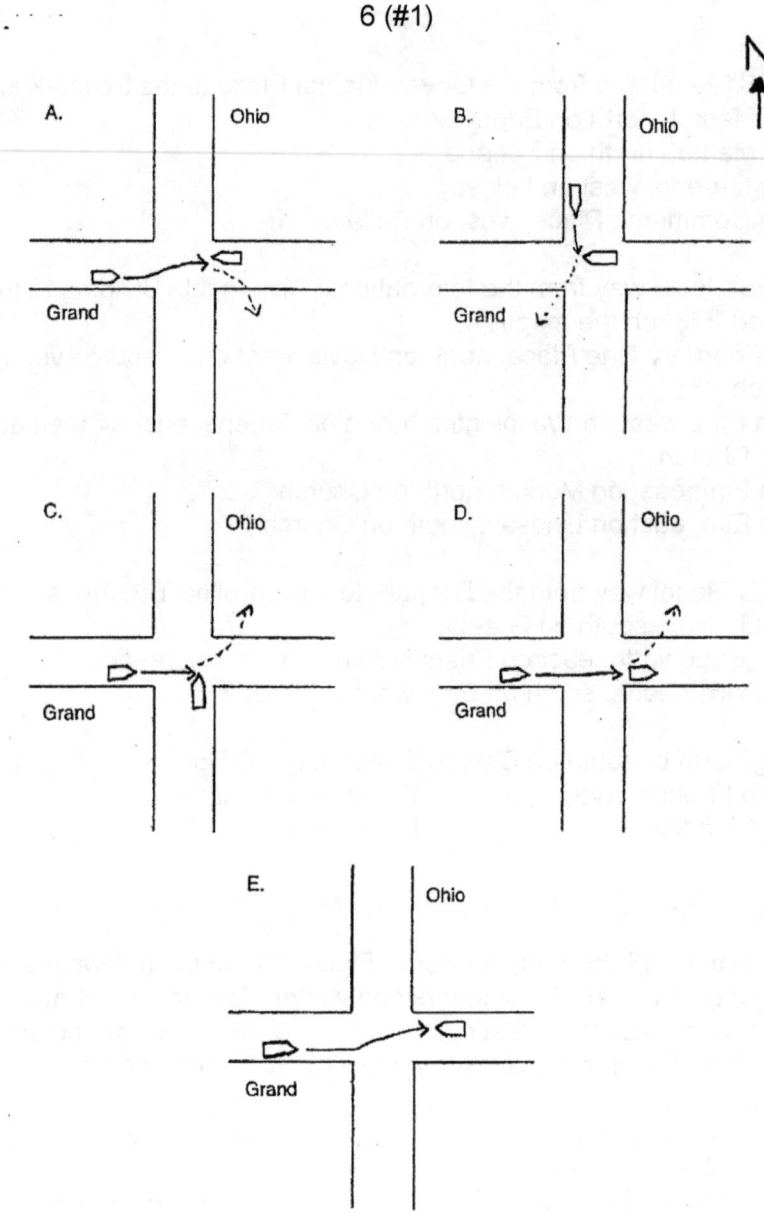

In the space at the right, print the letter of the drawing that BEST fit the descriptions written below.

15. A driver headed south on Ohio runs a red light and strikes the front of a car headed west on Grand. He glances off and leaves the roadway at the southwest corner of Grand and Ohio.   15._____

16. A driver heading east on Grand drifts into the oncoming lane as it travels through the intersection of Grand and Ohio, and strikes an oncoming car head-on   16._____

17. A driver heading east on Grand veers into the oncoming lane, sideswipes a westbound car and overcorrects as he swerves back into his lane. He leaves the roadway near the southeast corner of Grand and Ohio.

17.____

18. A driver heading east on Grand strikes the front of a car that is traveling north on Ohio and has run a red light. After striking the front of the northbound car, the driver veers left and leaves the roadway at the northeast corner of Grand and Ohio.

18.____

19. A driver heading east on Grand is traveling above the speed limit and clips the rear end of another eastbound car. The driver then veers to the left and leaves the roadway at the northeast corner of Grand and Ohio.

19.____

Questions 20-22.

DIRECTIONS: In Questions 20 through 22, choose the word or phrase CLOSEST in meaning to the word or phrase printed in capital letters.

20. PETITION
    A. appeal   B. law   C. oath   D. opposition

20.____

21. MALPRACTICE
    A. commission   B. mayhem   C. error   D. misconduct

21.____

22. EXONERATE
    A. incriminate   B. accuse   C. lengthen   D. acquit

22.____

Questions 23-25.

DIRECTIONS: Questions 23 through 25 measure your ability to do fieldwork-related arithmetic. Each question presents a separate arithmetic problem for you to solve.

23. Officers Lane and Bryant visited another city as part of an investigation. Because each is from a different precinct, they agree to split all expenses. With her credit card, Lane paid $70 for food and $150 for lodging. Bryant wrote checks for gas ($50) and entertainment ($40).
    How much does Bryant owe Lane?
    A. $65   B. $90   C. $155   D. $210

23.____

24. In a remote mountain pass, two search-and-rescue teams, one from Silverton and one from Durango, combine to look for a family that disappeared in a recent snowstorm. The combined team is composed of 20 members.
    Which of the following statements could NOT be true?
    A. The Durango team has a dozen members.
    B. The Silverton team has only one member.
    C. The Durango team has two more members than the Silverton team.
    D. The Silverton team has one more member than the Durango team.

24.____

25. Three people in the department share a vehicle for a period of one year. The average number of miles traveled per month by each person is 150. How many miles will be added to the car's odometer at the end of the year?   25._____
    A. 1,800   B. 2,400   C. 3,600   D. 5,400

KEY (CORRECT ANSWERS)

1.	D		11.	D
2.	C		12.	C
3.	A		13.	D
4.	A		14.	D
5.	A		15.	B
6.	A		16.	E
7.	B		17.	A
8.	C		18.	C
9.	B		19.	D
10.	D		20.	A

21. D
22. D
23. A
24. D
25. D

SOLUTIONS TO QUESTIONS 1-9

P implies Q = original statement

Not Q implies not P = contrapositive of the original statement. A statement and its contrapositive are logically equivalent.

Q implies P = converse of the original statement

Not P implies not Q = inverse of the original statement. The converse and inverse of an original statement are logically equivalent.

P implies Q = Not P or Q.

1. The CORRECT answer is D.
   In items I and II, each statement is the converses of the other. A converse of a statement is not equivalent to its original statement.

2. The CORRECT answer is C.
   In item I, the first statement is equivalent to "If Trilox is absent, then Rhopsin is also absent." But this does NOT imply that if Trilox is present, so too must Rhopsin be present. In item II, each statement is the contrapositive of the other. Thus, they are equivalent.

3. The CORRECT answer is A.
   In item I, the first sentence tells us that if a student is a sophomore, he/she will not go the prom. The second statement is equivalent to "If a student does attend the prom, he/she is not a sophomore." This is the contrapositive of the first statement, (so it is equivalent to it).

4. The CORRECT answer is A.
   In item I, the second statement can be written as "If the family sees their son again, then they must have paid the ransom." This is the contrapositive of the first statement. In item II, these statements are converses of each other; thus, they are not equivalent.

5. The CORRECT answer is A.
   If more than 365 babies were born in the county in one year, then at least two babies must share the same birthday.

6. The CORRECT answer is A.
   Given that most people who work for MetroLife are claims adjustors, plus the fact that all claims adjustors drive only a Ford sedan, it is a reasonable conclusion that any person who drives a Ford sedan and works for MetroLife is a claims adjustor.

7. The CORRECT answer is B.
   Jones will not speak to Zisk if Zisk will speak to Ronaldson, which will happen if Mason will speak to Zisk.

8. The CORRECT answer is C.
We are given that blue lights are never an indicator for the drive belt status. If some of the lights on the lower panel of the machine are blue, then it is reasonable to conclude that some of the lights on the lower panel are not indicators for the drive belt status.

9. The CORRECT answer is B.
There is only one sister that does not have brown eyes and only one sister that is not a doctor, and if the information in answer B is correct, then we learn that the same sister is a non-doctor without brown eyes. We also learn that this same non-doctor is not married. Since this all describes the same sister, we can conclude that two of the other sisters must be married doctors with brown eyes.

TEST 2

DIRECTIONS: Each question or incomplete statement is followed by several suggested answers or completions. Select the one that BEST answers the question or completes the statement. *PRINT THE LETTER OF THE CORRECT ANSWER IN THE SPACE AT THE RIGHT.*

Questions 1-9.

DIRECTIONS: Questions 1 through 9 measure your ability to (1) determine whether statements from witnesses say essentially the same thing and (2) determine the evidence needed to make it reasonably certain that a particular conclusion is true.
To do well on this part of the test, you do NOT have to have a working knowledge of police procedures and techniques. Nor do you have to have any more familiarity with criminals and criminal behavior than that acquired from reading newspapers, listening to radio or watching TV. To do well in this part, you must read and reason carefully.

1. Which of the following pairs of statements say essentially the same thing in two different ways?
   I. If there is life on Mars, we should fund NASA.
      Either there is life on Mars, or we should not fund NASA.
   II. All Eagle Scouts are teenage boys.
      All teenage boy are Eagle Scouts.
   The CORRECT answer is:
   A. I only   B. I and II   C. II only   D. Neither I nor II

2. Which of the following pairs of statements say essentially the same thing in two different ways?
   I. If that notebook is missing its front cover, it definitely belongs to Carter.
      Carter's notebook is the only one missing its front cover.
   II. If it's hot, the pool is open.
      The pool is open if it's hot.
   The CORRECT answer is:
   A. I only   B. I and II   C. II only   D. Neither I nor II

3. Which of the following pairs of statements say essentially the same thing in two different ways?
   I. Nobody who works at the mill is without benefits.
      Everyone who works at the mill has benefits.
   II. We will fund the program only if at least 100 people sign the petition.
      Either we will fund the program or at least 100 people will sign the petition.
   The CORRECT answer is:
   A. I only   B. I and II   C. II only   D. Neither I nor II

4. Which of the following pairs of statements say essentially the same thing in two different ways?
   I. If the new parts arrive, Mr. Luther's request has been answered.
      Mr. Luther requested new parts to arrive.
   II. The machine's test cycle will not run unless the operation cycle is not running.
      The machine's test cycle must be running in order for the operation cycle to run.
   The CORRECT answer is:
   A. I only   B. I and II   C. II only   D. Neither I nor II

5. Summary of Evidence Collected to Date:
   I. To become a member of the East Side Crips, a kid must be either "jumped in" or steal a squad car without getting caught.
   II. Sid, a kid on the East Side, was caught stealing a squad car.
   Prematurely Drawn Conclusion: Sid did not become a member of the East Side Crips.
   Which of the following pieces of evidence, if any, would make it reasonably certain that the conclusion drawn is true?
   A. "Jumping in" is not allowed in prison.
   B. Sid was not "jumped in."
   C. Sid's stealing the squad car had nothing to do with wanting to join the East Side Crips.
   D. None of the above

6. Summary of Evidence Collected to Date:
   I. Jones, a Precinct 8 officer, has more arrests than Smith.
   II. Smith and Watson have exactly the same number of arrests.
   Prematurely Drawn Conclusion: Watson is not a Precinct 8 officer.
   Which of the following pieces of evidence, if any, would make it reasonably certain that the conclusion drawn is true?
   A. All the officers in Precinct 8 have more arrests than Watson.
   B. All the officers in Precinct 8 have fewer arrests than Watson.
   C. Watson has fewer arrests than Jones.
   D. None of the above

7. Summary of Evidence Collected to Date:
   I. Twenty one-dollar bills are divided among Frances, Kerry, and Brian.
   II. If Kerry gives her dollar bills to Frances, then Frances will have more money than Brian.
   Prematurely Drawn Conclusion: Frances has twelve dollars.
   Which of the following pieces of evidence, if any, would make it reasonably certain that the conclusion drawn is true?
   A. If Brian gives his dollars to Kerry, then Kerry will have more money than Frances.
   B. Brian has two dollars.
   C. If Kerry gives her dollars to Brian, Brian will still have less money than Frances.
   D. None of the above

8. <u>Summary of Evidence Collected to Date</u>:
   I. The street sweepers will be here at noon today.
   II. Residents on the west side of the street should move their cars before noon.
   <u>Prematurely Drawn Conclusion</u>: Today is Wednesday.
   Which of the following pieces of evidence, if any, would make it reasonably certain that the conclusion drawn is true?
   A. The street sweepers never sweep the east side of the street on Wednesday.
   B. The street sweepers arrive at noon every other day.
   C. There is no parking allowed on the west side of the street on Wednesday.
   D. None of the above

8.____

9. <u>Summary of Evidence Collected to Date</u>:
   The only time the warning light comes on is when there is a power surge.
   <u>Prematurely Drawn Conclusion</u>: The warning light does not come on if the air conditioner is not running.
   Which of the following pieces of evidence, if any, would make it reasonably certain that the conclusion drawn is true?
   A. The air conditioner does not turn on if the warning light is on.
   B. Sometimes a power surge is caused by the dishwasher.
   C. There is only a power surge when the air conditioner turns on.
   D. None of the above

9.____

Questions 10-14.

DIRECTIONS: Questions 10 through 14 refer to Map #3 and measure your ability to orient yourself within a given section of town, neighborhood or particular area. Each of the questions describes a starting point and a destination. Assume that you are driving a car in the area shown on the map accompanying the questions. Use the map as a basis for the shortest way to get from one point to another without breaking the law.
On the map, a street marked by arrows, or by arrows and the words "One Way," indicates one-way travel and should be assumed to be one-way for the entire length, even when there are breaks or jogs in the street. EXCEPTION: A street that does not have the same name over the full length.

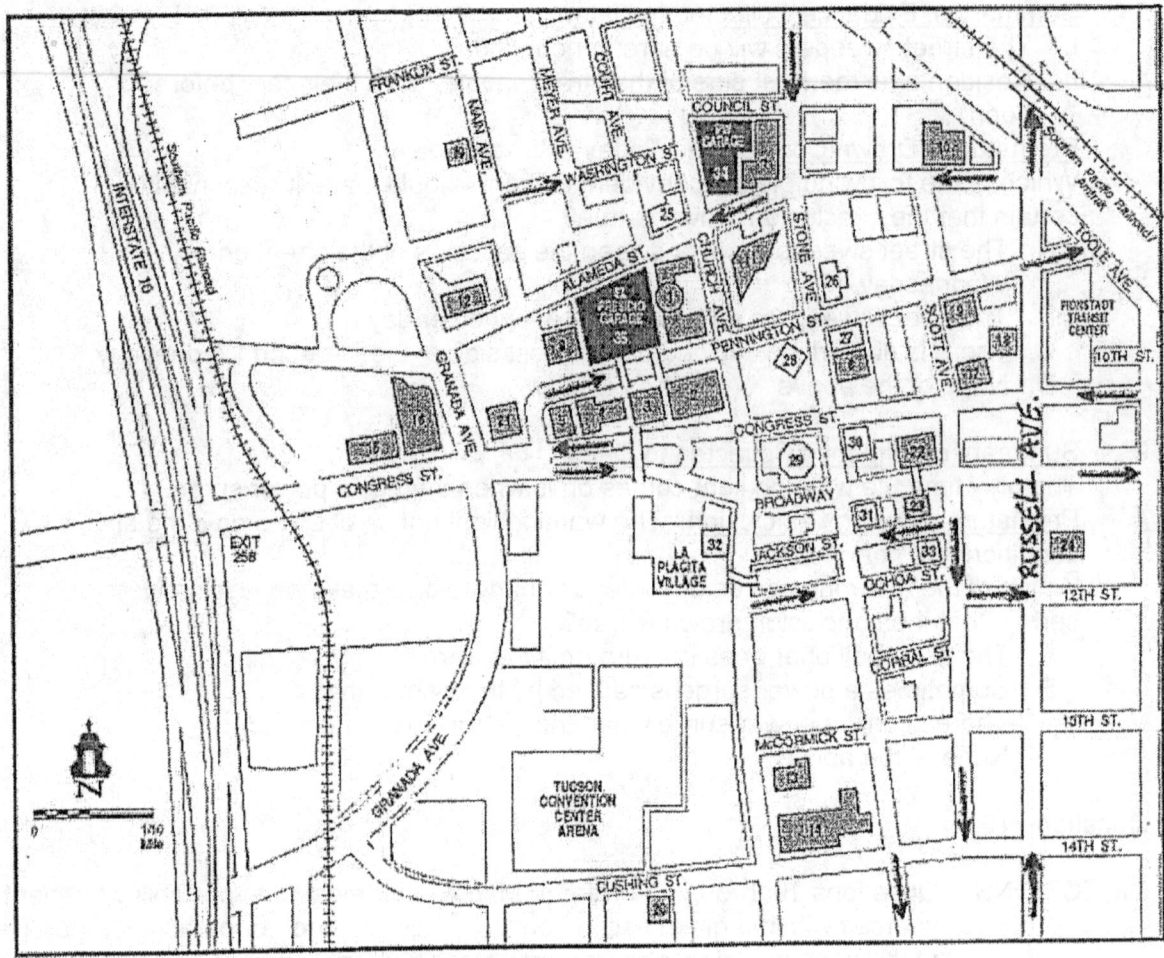

PIMA COUNTY
1. Old Courthouse
2. Superior Court Building
3. Administration Building
4. Health and Welfare Building
5. Mechanical Building
6. Legal Services Building
7. County/City Public Works Center

CITY OF TUCSON
8. City Hall
9. City Hall Annex
10. Alameda Plaza City Court Building
11. Public Library – Main Branch
12. Tucson Water Building
13. Fire Department Headquarters
14. Police Department Building

10. The SHORTEST legal way from the Public Library to the Alameda Plaza City Court Building is
    A. north on Stone Ave., east of Alameda
    B. south on Stone Ave., east on Congress, north on Russell Ave., west on Alameda
    C. south on Stone Ave., east on Pennington, north on Russell Ave., west on Alameda
    D. south on Church Ave., east on Pennington, north on Russell Ave., west on Alameda

10.____

11. The SHORTEST legal way from City Hall to the Police Department is   11.____
    A. east on Congress, south on Scott Ave., west on 14th
    B. east on Pennington, south on Stone Ave.
    C. east on Congress, south on Stone Ave.
    D. east on Pennington, south on Church Ave.

12. The SHORTEST legal way from the Tucson Water Building to the Legal Service   12.____
    Building is
    A. south on Granada Ave., east on Congress, north to east on Pennington, south on Stone Ave.
    B. east on Alameda, south on Church Ave., east on Pennington, south on Stone Ave.
    C. north on Granada Ave., east on Washington, south on Church Ave., east on Pennington, south on Stone Ave.
    D. south on Granada Ave., east on Cushing, north on Stone Ave.

13. The SHORTEST legal way from the Tucson Convention Center Arena to the   13.____
    City Hall Annex is
    A. west on Cushing, north on Granada Ave., east on Congress east on Broadway
    B. east on Cushing, north on Church Ave., east on Pennington
    C. east on Cushing, north on Russel Ave., west on Pennington
    D. east on Cushing, north on Stone Ave., east on Pennington

14. The SHORTEST legal way from Ronstadt Transit Center to the Fire Department   14.____
    is
    A. west on Pennington, south on Stone Ave., west on McCormick
    B. west on Congress, south on Russell Ave., west on 13th
    C. west on Congress, south on Church Ave.
    D. west on Pennington, south on Church Ave.

Questions 15-19.

DIRECTIONS: Questions 15 through 19 refer to Figure #3, on the following page, and measure your ability to understand written descriptions of events. Each question presents a description of an accident or event and asks you which of the following five drawings in Figure #3 BEST represents it.
In the drawings, the following symbols are used:
Moving vehicle ⌂   Non-moving vehicle ▲
Pedestrian or bicyclist •
The path and direction of travel of a vehicle or pedestrian is indicated by a solid line.
The path and direction of travel of each vehicle or pedestrian directly involved in a collision from the point of impact is indicated by a dotted line.

In the space at the right, print the letter of the drawing that BEST fit the descriptions written below.

6 (#2)

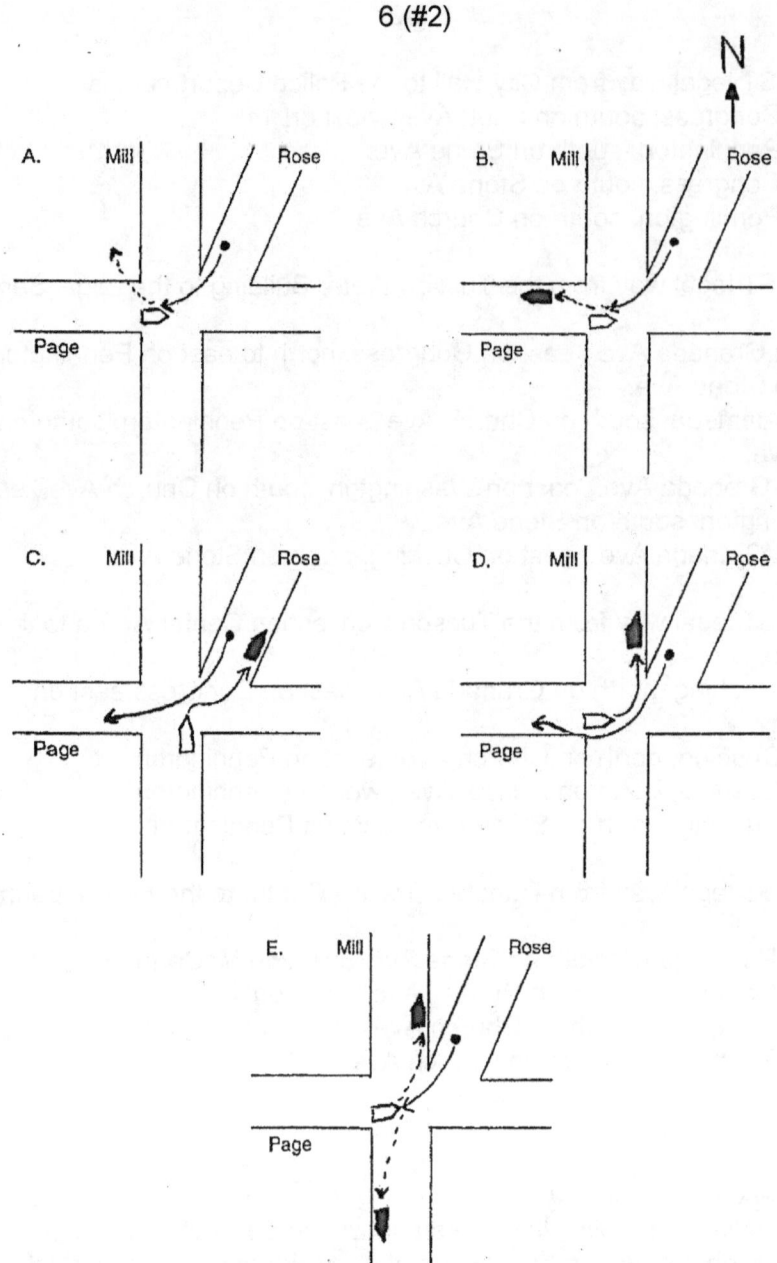

15. A bicyclist heading southwest on Rose travels into the intersection, sideswipes a car that is heading east on Page, and veers right, leaving the roadway at the northwest corner of Page and Mill.

15.____

16. A driver traveling north on Mill swerves right to avoid a bicyclist that is traveling southwest on Rose. The driver strikes the rear end of a car parked on Rose. The bicyclist continues through the intersection and travels west on Page.

16.____

17. A bicyclist heading southwest on Rose travels into the intersection, sideswipes a car that is heading east on Page, and veers right, striking the rear end of a car parked in the westbound lane on Page.

17.____

18. A driver traveling east on Page swerves left to avoid a bicyclist that is traveling   18.____
    southwest on Rose. The driver strikes the rear end of a car parked on Mill.
    The bicyclist continues through the intersection and travels west on Page.

19. A bicyclist heading southwest on Rose enters the intersection and sideswipes   19.____
    a car that is swerving left to avoid her. The bicyclist veers left and collides with
    a car parked in the southbound lane on Mill. The driver of the car veers left
    and collides with a car parked in the northbound lane on Mill.

Questions 20-22.

DIRECTIONS: In Questions 20 through 22, choose the word or phrase CLOSEST in meaning
              to the word or phrase printed in capital letters.

20. WAIVE   20.____
    A. cease   B. surrender   C. prevent   D. die

21. DEPOSITION   21.____
    A. settlement   B. deterioration C. testimony   D. character

22. IMMUNITY   22.____
    A. exposure   B. accusation   C. protection   D. exchange

Questions 23-25.

DIRECTIONS: Questions 23 through 25 measure your ability to do fieldwork-related
              arithmetic. Each question presents a separate arithmetic problem for you to
              solve.

23. Dean, a claims investigator, is reading a 445-page case record in his spare   23.____
    time at work. He has already read 157 pages.
    If Dean reads 24 pages a day, he should finish reading the rest of the record in
    ____ days.
    A. 7   B. 12   C. 19   D. 24

24. The Fire Department owns four cars. The Department of Sanitation owns twice   24.____
    as many cars as the Fire Department. The Department of Parks and
    Recreation owns one fewer car than the Department of Sanitation. The
    Department of Parks and Recreation is buying new tires for each of its cars.
    Each tire costs $100.
    How much is the Department of Parks and Recreation going to spend on tires?
    A. $400   B. $2,800   C. $3,200   D. $4,900

25. A dance hall is about 5,000 square feet. The local ordinance does not allow   25.____
    more than 50 people per every 100 square feet of commercial space.
    The maximum capacity of the hall is
    A. 500   B. 2,500   C. 5,000   D. 25,000

KEY (CORRECT ANSWERS)

1.	D		11.	D
2.	B		12.	A
3.	A		13.	B
4.	D		14.	C
5.	B		15.	A
6.	D		16.	C
7.	D		17.	B
8.	A		18.	D
9.	C		19.	E
10.	C		20.	B

21. C
22. C
23. B
24. B
25. B

SOLUTIONS TO QUESTIONS 1-9

P implies Q = original statement

Not Q implies not P = contrapositive of the original statement. A statement and its contrapositive are logically equivalent.

Q implies P = converse of the original statement

Not P implies not Q = inverse of the original statement. The converse and inverse of an original statement are logically equivalent.

P implies Q = Not P or Q.

1. The CORRECT answer is D.
   For item I, the second statement should be "Either there is no life on Mars or we should fund NASA" in order to be logically equivalent to the first statement. For item II, the statements are converses of each other; thus, they are not equivalent.

2. The CORRECT answer is B.
   In item I, this is an example of P implies Q and Q implies P. In this case, P = the notebook is missing its cover and Q = the notebook belongs to Carter. In item II, the ordering of the words is changed, but the If P then Q is exactly the same. P = it is hot and Q = the pool is open.

3. The CORRECT answer is A.
   For item I, if nobody is without benefits, then everybody has benefits. For item II, the second equivalent statement should be "either we will not fund the program or at least 100 people will sign the petition."

4. The CORRECT answer is D.
   For item I, the first statement is an implication, whereas the second statement mentions only one part of the implication (new parts are requested) and says nothing about the other part. For item II, the first statement is equivalent to "if the operating cycle is not running, then the test cycle will run." The second statement is equivalent to "if the operating cycle is running, then the test cycle will run." So, these statements in item II are not equivalent.

5. The CORRECT answer is B.
   Since Sid did not steal a car and avoid getting caught, the only other way he could become a Crips member would be "jumped in." Choice B tells us that Sid was not "jumped in," so we conclude that he did not become a member of the Crips.

6. The CORRECT answer is D.
   Since Smith and Watson have the same number of arrests, Watson must have fewer arrests than Jones. This means that each of choices A and B is impossible. Choice C would also not reveal whether or not Watson is a Precinct 8 officer.

10 (#2)

7. The CORRECT answer is D.
Exact dollar amounts still cannot be ascertained by using any of the other choices.

8. The CORRECT answer is A.
The street sweepers never sweep on the east side of the street on Wednesday; however, they will be here at noon today. This implies that they will sweep on the west side of the street. Since the residents should move their cars before noon, we can conclude that today is Wednesday.

9. The CORRECT answer is C.
We start with W implies P, where W = warning light comes on and P = power surge. Choice C would read as P implies A, where A = air conditioning is running. Combining these statements leads to W implies A. The conclusion can be read as: Not A implies Not W, which is equivalent to W implies A.

VISUAL SCANNING
MAP READING

COMMENTARY

This is a test of your ability to orient yourself within a given section or neighborhood of a city or community. In each problem, you are in a vehicle, and you are to choose the shortest way to get from one location to another without breaking any laws. In order to solve each problem, you will need to study the map accompanying each set of four problems. Always begin with the first problem in the set. The starting point for the vehicle in the first problem will be marked by the symbol ➡. On the sample map below, the vehicle is heading east on Scott. You will be asked to find your way from the first location to the second location. Each location will be marked with an X. Some of the streets on the map are one-way streets. An arrow ⇨ shows the direction in which you may travel on a street. If there is no arrow, you may travel in either direction. These maps are NOT real. Do not confuse them with any area you may know. Below is a sample problem

SAMPLE QUESTION

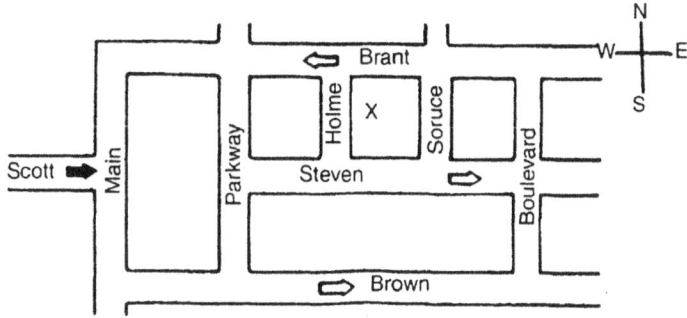

You are on Scott, and you are going to Holme. What is the MOST direct way to get there without breaking the law?
You are on Scott, and you are going to Holme. What is the MOST direct way to get there without breaking the law?
    A. Go right on Main, left on Brown, left on Boulevard, left on Steven, right on Holme to telephone
    B. Go left on Main, right on Brant, right on Holme to telephone
    C. Go right on Main, left on Brown, left on Parkway, right on Steven, left on Holme to telephone
    D. Go right on Main, left on Brown, left on Boulevard, left on Brant, left on Holme to telephone

The MOST direct way to get from the starting point to the location without breaking the law is described in choice C. Therefore, you would have marked C in the space at the right.

EXAMINATION SECTION
TEST 1

DIRECTIONS: Each map will be followed by several questions. For each question, you will be asked to go from one street to another street. There is ONLY ONE viable selection for each question, although it may not be the shortest route. Any street marked with either a ➡ or a ⬅ is a one-way street. Unmarked streets are two-ways.
In some cases, a PARTICULAR location on a street is mentioned in the question. This information should be used in arriving at a correct answer. All maps are hypothetical. *PRINT THE LETTER OF THE CORRECT ANSWER IN THE SPACE AT THE RIGHT.*

Questions 1-5.

DIRECTIONS: For Questions 1 to 5, use the following map.

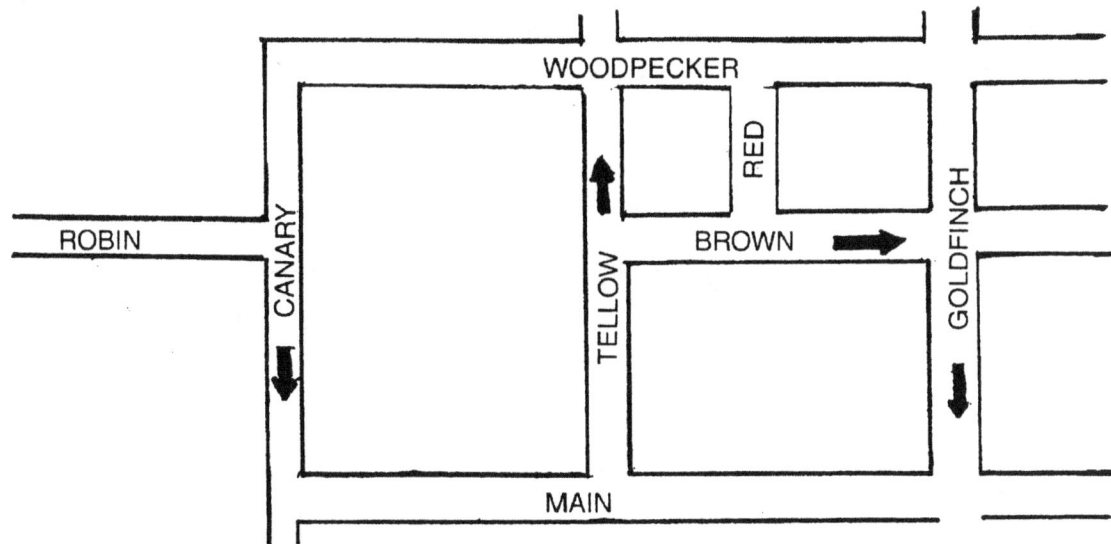

1. From Brown (east of Red) to Robin.

   A. Left on Goldfinch, left on Woodpecker, left on Canary, right on Robin
   B. Right on Goldfinch, right on Main, right on Yellow, left on Woodpecker, left on Canary, right on Robin
   C. Right on Goldfinch, right on Main, right on Canary, left on Robin
   D. Right on Goldfinch, left on Main, right on Canary, right on Robin

   1.____

2. From Canary to Red.

   A. Left on Main, left on Goldfinch, left on Woodpecker, left on Red
   B. Left on Main, left on Yellow, left on Woodpecker, right on Red
   C. Left on Main, left on Yellow, right on Brown, left on Red
   D. Right on Main, left on Goldfinch, left on Brown, right on Red

   2.____

2 (#1)

3. From Woodpecker (west of Yellow) to Brown.

   A. Left on Canary, left on Main, left on Yellow, right on Robin
   B. Right on Yellow, left on Brown
   C. Right on Yellow, left on Main, left on Goldfinch, right on Brown
   D. Right on Goldfinch, left on Brown

3.____

4. From Robin to Goldfinch.

   A. Right on Canary, left on Main, left on Goldfinch
   B. Left on Canary, right on Woodpecker, right on Goldfinch
   C. Right on Canary, left on Main, left on Yellow, right on Brown, right on Goldfinch
   D. Right on Canary, left on Main, right on Yellow, left on Brown, left on Goldfinch

4.____

5. From Red to Main.

   A. Left on Brown, left on Goldfinch, left on Main
   B. Right on Brown, right on Yellow, left on Woodpecker, right on Canary, left on Main
   C. Right on Brown, left on Yellow, right on Main
   D. Left on Brown, right on Goldfinch, right on Main

5.____

Questions 6-11.

DIRECTIONS: For Questions 6 to 11, use the following map.

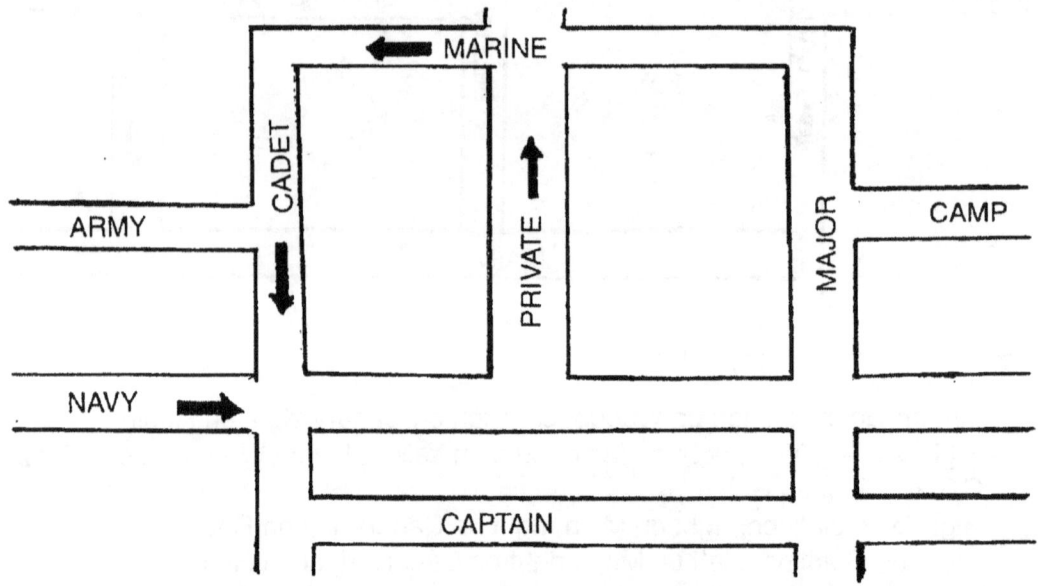

6. From Army to Camp.

   A. Right on Cadet, left on Navy, right on Major, right on Camp
   B. Left on Cadet, left on Marine, right on Major, left on Camp
   C. Right on Cadet, left on Navy, left on Major, right on Camp
   D. Right on Cadet, right on Navy, left on Major, left on Camp

6.____

7. From Captain to Marine.

   A. Left on Major, left on Marine
   B. Left on Major, left on Navy, right on Private, left on Marine

7.____

100

C. Right on Cadet, right on Marine
D. Right on Cadet, right on Navy, left on Private, left on Marine

8. From Navy (between Private and Major) to Cadet.

    A. Right on Major, right on Captain, right on Cadet
    B. Right on Private, left on Marine, right on Cadet
    C. Left on Major, left on Marine, left on Cadet
    D. Right on Captain, right on Navy, right on Cadet

8.____

9. From Navy (west of Cadet) to Array.

    A. Left on Private, left on Marine, left on Cadet, right on Army
    B. Left on Private, right on Marine, right on Army
    C. Left on Cadet, left on Army
    D. Right on Major, right on Captain, right on Cadet, left on Army

9.____

10. From Major to Army.

    A. Right on Navy, right on Cadet, right on Army
    B. Right on Captain, right on Cadet, left on Army
    C. Right on Navy, right on Private, left on Marine left on Cadet, right on Army
    D. Left on Marine, left on Cadet, right on Army

10.____

11. From Private to Captain.

    A. Right on Marine, right on Major, right on Captain
    B. Left on Navy, left on Major, right on Captain
    C. Left on Marine, left on Cadet, left on Captain
    D. Left on Marine, left on Cadet, left on Navy, left on Major, right on Captain

11.____

Questions 12-18.

DIRECTIONS: For Questions 12 to 18, use the following map.

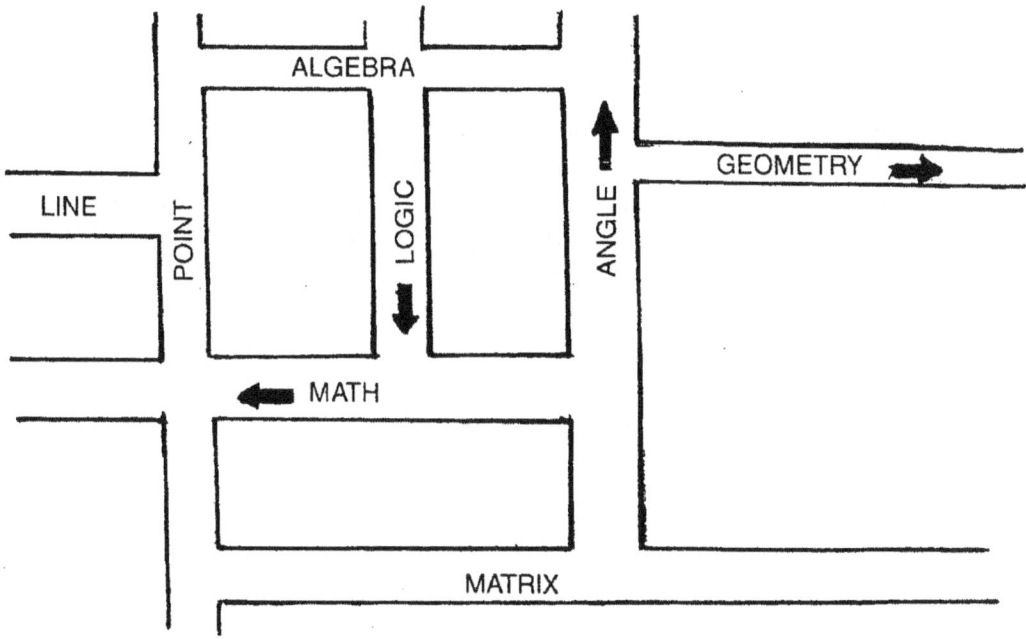

12. From Math to Angle (north of Algebra). 12.____
    A. Left on Point, right on Matrix, left on Angle
    B. Right on Point, right on Algebra, left on Angle
    C. Right on Logic, right on Algebra, left on Angle
    D. Left on Logic, left on Matrix, left on Angle

13. From Algebra to Geometry. 13.____
    A. Left on Logic, left on Math, right on Angle, right on Geometry
    B. Right on Point, left on Matrix, left on Angle, right on Geometry
    C. Left on Logic, right on Math, right on Point, right on Algebra, right on Angle, left on Geometry
    D. Left on Point, left on Matrix, left on Angle, right on Geometry

14. From Line to Logic. 14.____
    A. Left on Point, right on Algebra, right on Logic
    B. Right on Point, left on Math, left on Logic
    C. Left on Point, left on Algebra, right on Logic
    D. Right on Point, left on Matrix, right on Angle, left on Math, right on Logic

15. From Angle (between Math and Algebra) to Point. 15.____
    A. Left on Math, right on Point
    B. Left on Algebra, left on Point
    C. Left on Matrix, right on Point
    D. Left on Logic, right on Math, left on Point

16. From Matrix to Algebra. 16.____
    A. Right on Point, right on Math, left on Angle, left on Algebra
    B. Right on Angle, left on Algebra
    C. Right on Point, right on Algebra
    D. Left on Math, left on Point, right on Algebra

17. From Line to Geometry. 17.____
    A. Left on Point, right on Algebra, right on Angle, left on Geometry
    B. Right on Point, left on Math, left on Angle, right on Geometry
    C. Left on Point, left on Algebra, right on Logic, left on Angle, right on Geometry
    D. Right on Point, left on Matrix, left on Angle, right on Geometry

18. From Logic to Matrix. 18.____
    A. Right on Math, left on Point, left on Matrix
    B. Right on Math, right on Point, right on Matrix
    C. Left on Math, left on Angle, left on Matrix
    D. Right on Algebra, right on Angle, right on Matrix

Questions 19-25.

DIRECTIONS: For Questions 19 to 25, use the following map.

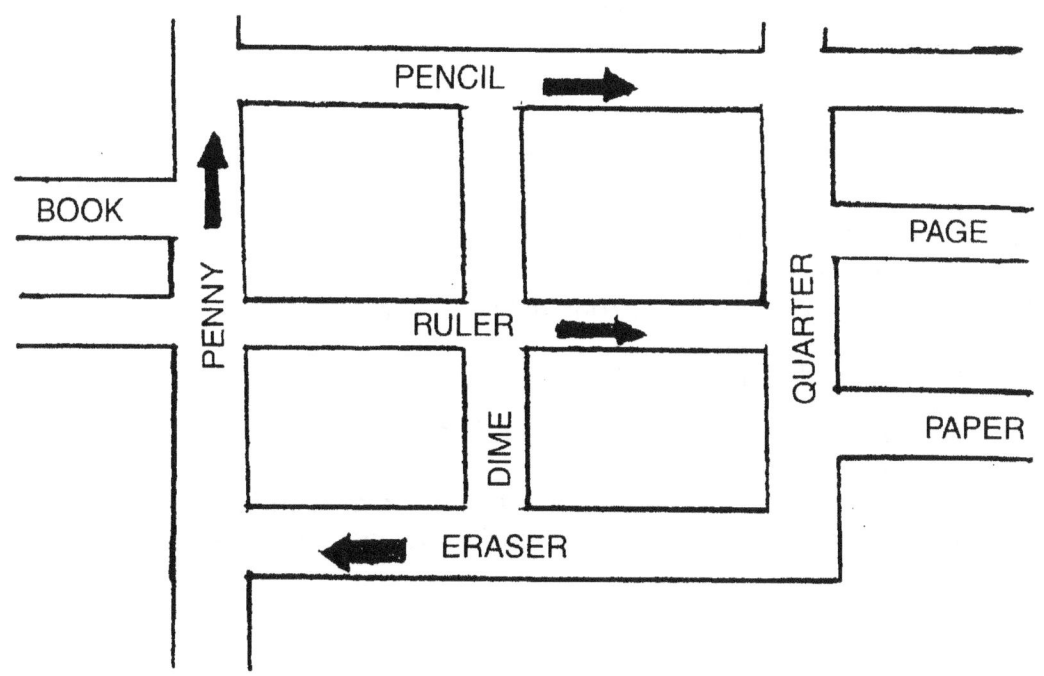

19. From Page to Dime.

    A. Right on Quarter, left on Pencil, left on Dime
    B. Left on Quarter, right on Ruler, right on Dime
    C. Right on Quarter, right on Pencil, left on Dime
    D. Left on Quarter, right on Eraser, right on Dime

19.____

20. From Penny to Eraser (between Dime and Quarter).

    A. Right on Pencil, right on Quarter, right on Eraser
    B. Right on Pencil, right on Dime, right on Eraser
    C. Right on Ruler, left on Quarter, right on Eraser
    D. Left on Ruler, right on Dime, right on Eraser

20.____

21. From Book to Quarter (south of Paper).

    A. Right on Penny, left on Ruler, right on Quarter
    B. Left on Penny, right on Ruler, right on Quarter
    C. Right on Penny, left on Eraser, left on Quarter
    D. Left on Penny, right on Pencil, right on Quarter

21.____

22. From Paper to Pencil (west of Dime).

    A. Right on Quarter, left on Pencil
    B. Left on Quarter, right on Eraser, right on Penny, right on Pencil
    C. Right on Quarter, right on Eraser, right on Dime, right on Pencil
    D. Left on Quarter, right on Eraser, right on Dime, left on Pencil

22.____

23. From Pencil (between Dime and Quarter) to Book.

    A. Right on Dime, right on Eraser, left on Penny, left on Book
    B. Right on Quarter, right on Ruler, right on Penny, left on Book
    C. Right on Quarter, right on Eraser, right on Penny, left on Book
    D. Right on Dime, right on Ruler, left on Book

24. From Penny (south of Eraser) to Dime (north of Ruler).

    A. Right on Ruler, left on Dime
    B. Right on Ruler, right on Dime
    C. Right on Pencil, left on Dime
    D. Right on Pencil, right on Quarter, right on Dime

25. From Ruler (west of Penny) to Paper.

    A. Right on Dime, left on Eraser, right on Paper
    B. Right on Quarter, left on Paper
    C. Left on Penny, right on Pencil, right on Quarter, right on Paper
    D. Right on Penny, left on Eraser, left on Quarter, right on Paper

---

KEY (CORRECT ANSWERS)

1.	B		11.	C
2.	C		12.	B
3.	A		13.	D
4.	C		14.	A
5.	D		15.	B
6.	C		16.	C
7.	A		17.	D
8.	C		18.	A
9.	A		19.	D
10.	D		20.	A

21. D
22. B
23. C
24. A
25. B

TEST 2

DIRECTIONS: Each map will be followed by several questions. For each question, you will be asked to go from one street to another street. There is ONLY ONE viable selection for each question, although it may not be the shortest route. Any street marked with either a ➡ or a ⬅ is a one-way street. Unmarked streets are two-ways.
In some cases, a PARTICULAR location on a street is mentioned in the question. This information should be used in arriving at a correct answer. All maps are hypothetical. *PRINT THE LETTER OF THE CORRECT ANSWER IN THE SPACE AT THE RIGHT.*

Questions 1-6.

DIRECTIONS: For Questions 1 to 6, use the following map.

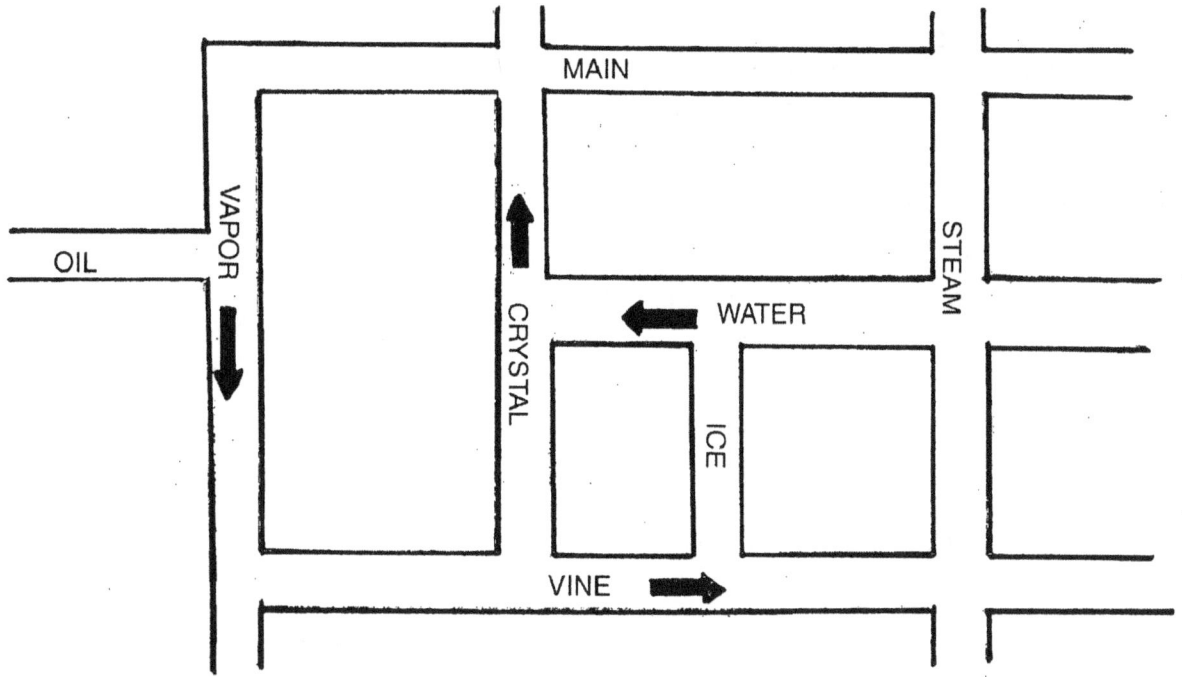

1. From Steam (north of Water) to Ice.

    A. Right on Water, left on Ice
    B. Right on Water, left on Crystal, left on Vine, left on Ice
    C. Left on Main, left on Crystal, right on Vine, right on Ice
    D. Left on Main, right on Vapor, left on Vine, right on Ice

2. From Oil to Main (east of Crystal).

    A. Right on Vapor, right on Crystal, left on Main
    B. Left on Vapor, right on Main
    C. Right on Vapor, left on Vine, left on Crystal, right on Main
    D. Left on Vapor, right on Vine, left on Main

105

3. From Water to Oil.

    A. Right on Crystal, left on Vapor, right on Oil
    B. Left on Crystal, right on Vine, right on Vapor, left on Oil
    C. Right on Crystal, left on Main, left on Vapor, right on Oil
    D. Left on Ice, right on Vapor, left on Oil

4. From Vine (between Crystal and Ice) to Crystal.

    A. Left on Ice, right on Steam, left on Crystal
    B. Left on Ice, left on Water, right on Crystal
    C. Left on Ice, right on Water, left on Crystal
    D. Left on Ice, left on Steam, right on Crystal

5. From Main (between Crystal and Steam) to Vine (east of Ice).

    A. Left on Crystal, left on Vine
    B. Right on Steam, right on Vine
    C. Right on Steam, right on Water, left on Ice, left on Vine
    D. Right on Steam, right on Water, right on Crystal, right on Vine

6. From Ice to Crystal (south of Water).

    A. Left on Water, left on Crystal
    B. Right on Water, left on Steam, left on Main, left on Crystal
    C. Right on Vine, right on Crystal
    D. Left on Water, right on Crystal, left on Main, left on Vapor, left on Vine, left oh Crystal

Questions 7-12.

DIRECTIONS: For Questions 7 to 12, use the following map.

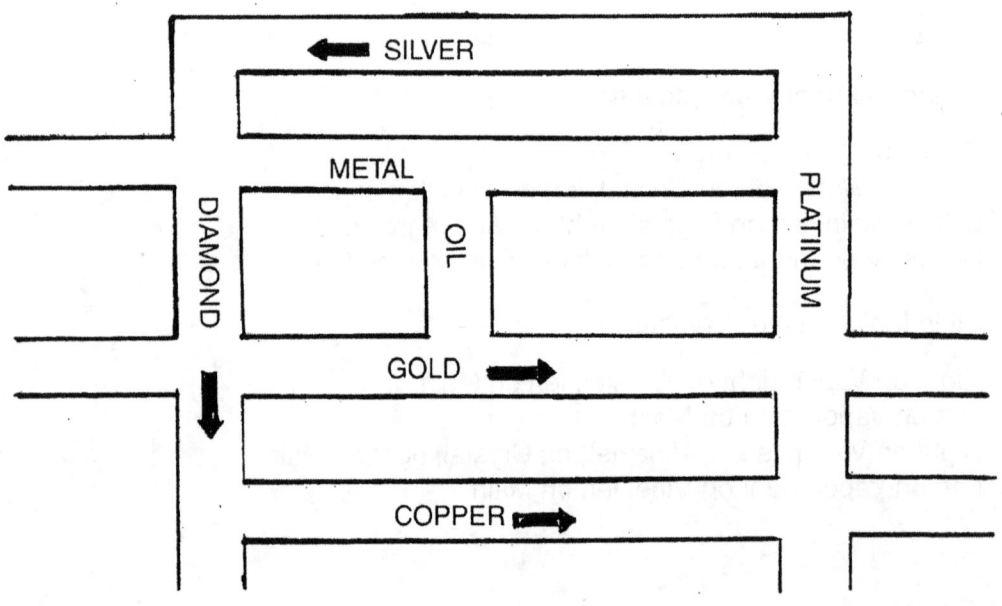

7. From Copper (west of Platinum) to Oil. 7.____
    A. Right on Diamond, right on Metal, right on Oil
    B. Left on Platinum, left on Gold, right on Oil
    C. Right on Diamond, right on Gold, left on Oil
    D. Left on Platinum, left on Metal, left on Oil

8. From Silver to Platinum (south of Copper). 8.____
    A. Left on Diamond, left on Gold, right on Platinum
    B. Left on Diamond, left on Copper, left on Platinum
    C. Right on Metal, left on Platinum
    D. Left on Diamond, left on Gold, left on Platinum

9. From Oil to Diamond (north of Metal). 9.____
    A. Left on Metal, left on Diamond
    B. Right on Gold, right on Diamond
    C. Left on Metal, right on Diamond
    D. Left on Gold, right on Copper, left on Diamond

10. From Platinum (between Gold and Copper) to Gold (between Oil and Diamond) 10.____
    A. Left on Metal, left on Oil, left on Gold
    B. Left on Silver, right on Diamond, right on Gold
    C. Left on Metal, left on Diamond, left on Gold
    D. Left on Silver, left on Oil, right on Gold

11. From Metal (west of Diamond) to Silver. 11.____
    A. Left on Diamond, right on Silver
    B. Left on Platinum, left on Silver
    C. Right on Platinum, right on Silver
    D. Right on Diamond, left on Silver

12. From Diamond (south of Copper) to Diamond (north of Metal). 12.____
    A. Right on Copper, left on Platinum, left on Silver, left on Diamond
    B. Right on Gold, left on Oil, left on Metal, left on Diamond
    C. Right on Copper, left on Platinum, left on Metal, right on Diamond
    D. Right on Copper, left on Platinum, left on Gold, right on Diamond

Questions 13-21.

DIRECTIONS: For Questions 13 to 21, use the following map.

4 (#2)

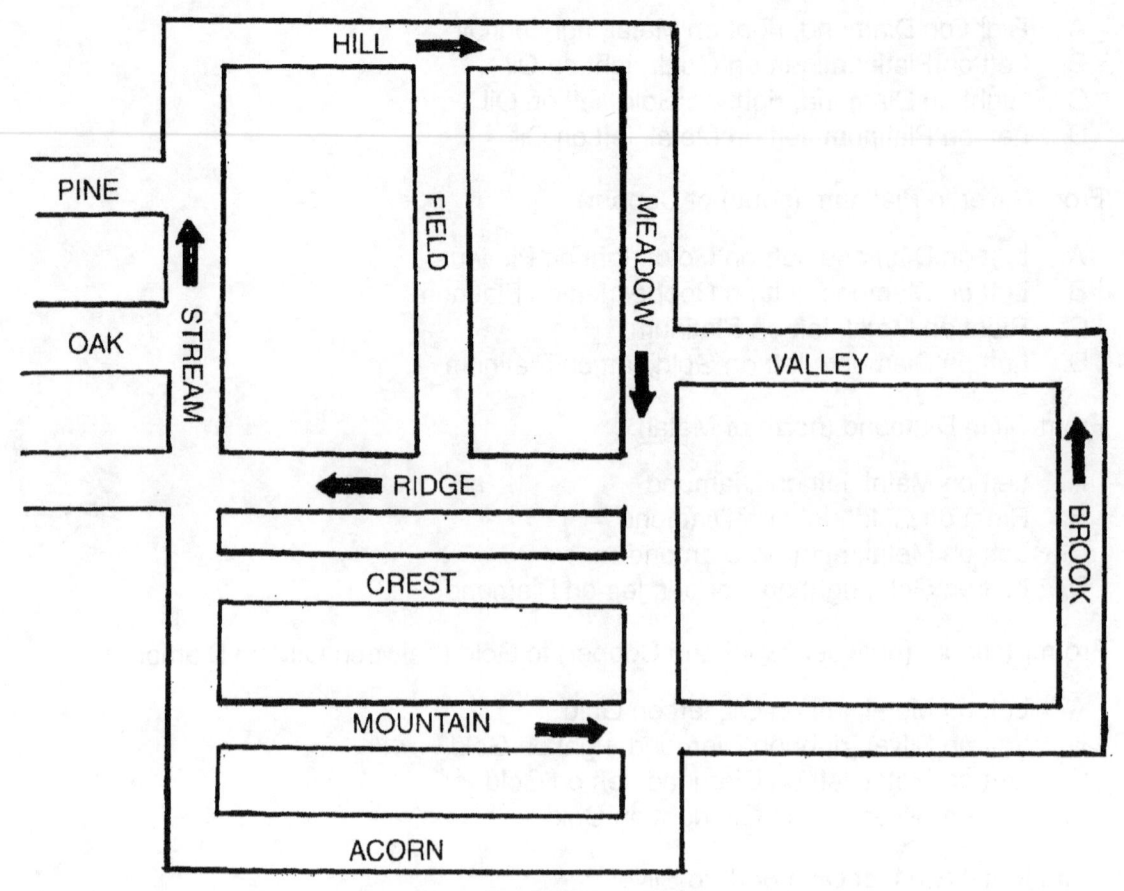

13. From Crest to Field.

   A. Left on Meadow, left on Ridge, right on Field
   B. Right on Stream, right on Hill, left on Field
   C. Right on Meadow, right on Ridge, left on Field
   D. Right on Stream, right on Hill, right on Field

14. From Valley to Oak.

   A. Left on Meadow, right on Mountain, left on Stream, left on Oak
   B. Left on Meadow, right on Ridge, right on Stream, left on Oak
   C. Right on Meadow, left on Hill, left on Stream, right on Oak
   D. Left on Meadow, left on Crest, right on Stream, left on Oak

15. From Field to Mountain (east of Meadow).

   A. Right on Hill, right on Meadow, left on Mountain
   B. Right on Ridge, right on Stream, left on Mountain
   C. Left on Ridge, right on Meadow, right on Mountain
   D. Right on Hill, left on Stream, right on Mountain

16. From Pine to Ridge (east of Field).

   A. Left on Stream, right on Hill, right on Field, right on Ridge
   B. Right on Stream, left on Ridge

      C. Left on Stream, left on Field, left on Ridge
      D. Left on Stream, right on Hill, right on Meadow, right on Ridge

17. From Brook to Mountain (west of Meadow).

      A. Left on Valley, left on Meadow, right on Acorn, right on Stream, right on Mountain
      B. Left on Valley, left on Meadow, right on Mountain
      C. Left on Valley, right on Meadow, right on Ridge, left on Stream, left on Mountain
      D. Left on Meadow, right on Mountain

18. From Acorn to Meadow (between Crest and Ridge).

      A. Right on Stream, right on Mountain, left on Meadow
      B. Left on Stream, left on Crest, right on Meadow
      C. Right on Stream, right on Hill, right on Meadow
      D. Right on Stream, right on Crest, right on Meadow

19. From Ridge (east of Field) to Brook.

      A. Right on Meadow, left on Mountain, left on Brook
      B. Left on Stream, left on Crest, right on Meadow, left on Mountain, left on Brook
      C. Left on Meadow, right on Valley, right on Brook
      D. Right on Field, right on Hill, right on Meadow, left on Mountain, left on Brook

20. From Meadow (between Crest and Mountain) to Oak.

      A. Right on Acorn, right on Stream, left on Oak
      B. Right on Crest, right on Stream, left on Oak
      C. Right on Mountain, right on Stream, left on Oak
      D. Left on Hill, left on Stream, right on Oak

21. From Acorn to Ridge (west of Field).

      A. Left on Meadow, left on Ridge
      B. Right on Mountain, left on Brook, left on Valley, right on Meadow, left on Ridge
      C. Right on Stream, right on Hill, right on Field, right on Ridge
      D. Right on Stream, right on Mountain, left on Meadow, left on Ridge

Questions 22-25.

DIRECTIONS: For Questions 22 to 25, use the following map.

6 (#2)

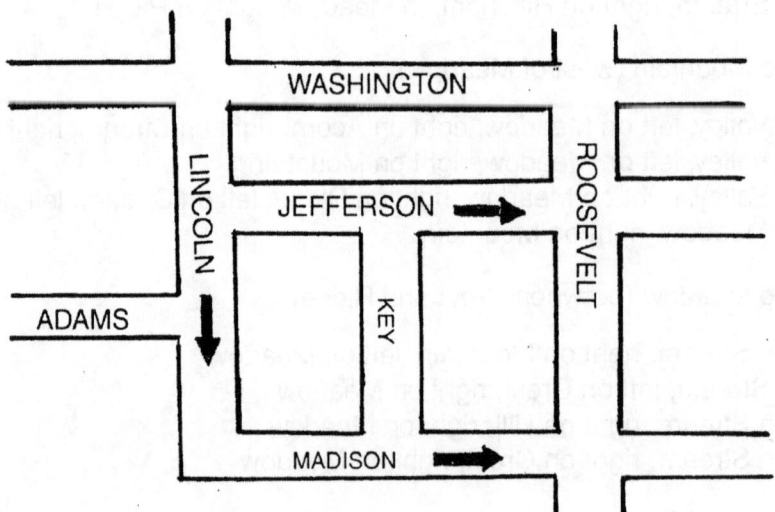

22. From Roosevelt (south of Madison) to Adams.

   A. Left on Washington, right on Lincoln, right on Adams
   B. Left on Jefferson, left on Lincoln, right on Adams
   C. Left on Washington, left on Lincoln, right on Adams
   D. Right on Jefferson, right on Key, right on Lincoln, left on Adams

23. From Madison (west of Key) to Jefferson (east of Roosevelt).

   A. Left on Roosevelt, left on Jefferson
   B. Left on Key, right on Jefferson
   C. Left on Key, left on Jefferson
   D. Left on Roosevelt, right on Washington, right on Jefferson

24. From Lincoln (south of Jefferson) to Adams.

   A. Right on Jefferson, right on Key, right on Madison, left on Adams
   B. Left on Jefferson, left on Lincoln, right on Adams
   C. Left on Washington, right on Lincoln, left on Adams
   D. Left on Madison, left on Roosevelt, left on Washington, left on Lincoln, right on Adams

25. From Washington (between Lincoln and Roosevelt) to Key.

   A. Right on Lincoln, left on Jefferson, right on Key
   B. Right on Roosevelt, right on Jefferson, left on Key
   C. Right on Roosevelt, right on Madison, right on Key
   D. Left on Lincoln, left on Madison, left on Key

KEY (CORRECT ANSWERS)

1. A
2. C
3. C
4. B
5. C

6. D
7. D
8. A
9. C
10. C

11. B
12. A
13. D
14. B
15. A

16. D
17. A
18. C
19. D
20. A

21. C
22. C
23. B
24. D
25. D

PREPARING WRITTEN MATERIALS
EXAMINATION SECTION
TEST 1

DIRECTIONS: Each question consists of a sentence which may be classified appropriately under one of the following four categories:
A. Incorrect because of faulty grammar or sentence structure.
B. Incorrect because of faulty punctuation.
C. Incorrect because of faulty spelling or capitalization.
D. Correct

Examine each sentence carefully. Then, in the space at the right, print the capital letter preceding the option which is the BEST of the four suggested above. All incorrect sentences contain only one type of error. Consider a sentence correct if it contains none of the types of errors mentioned, although there may be other correct ways of expressing the same thought.

1. The fire apparently started in the storeroom, which is usually locked. 1.____
2. On approaching the victim two bruises were noticed by this officer. 2.____
3. The officer, who was there examined the report with great care. 3.____
4. Each employee in the office had a separate desk. 4.____
5. The suggested procedure is similar to the one now in use. 5.____
6. No one was more pleased with the new procedure than the chauffeur. 6.____
7. He tried to pursuade her to change the procedure. 7.____
8. The total of the expenses charged to petty cash were high. 8.____
9. An understanding between him and I was finally reached. 9.____
10. It was at the supervisor's request that the clerk agreed to postpone his vacation. 10.____
11. We do not believe that it is necessary for both he and the clerk to attend the conference. 11.____
12. All employees, who display perseverance, will be given adequate recognition. 12.____
13. He regrets that some of us employees are dissatisfied with our new assignments. 13.____

14. "Do you think that the raise was merited," asked the supervisor?   14._____

15. The new manual of procedure is a valuable supplament to our rules and regulation.   15._____

16. The typist admitted that she had attempted to pursuade the other employees to assist her in her work.   16._____

17. The supervisor asked that all amendments to the regulations be handled by you and I.   17._____

18. They told both he and I that the prisoner had escaped.   18._____

19. Any superior officer, who, disregards the just complaints of his subordinates, is remiss in the performance of his duty.   19._____

20. Only those members of the national organization who resided in the Middle west attended the conference in Chicago.   20._____

21. We told him to give the investigation assignment to whoever was available.   21._____

22. Please do not disappoint and embarass us by not appearing in court.   22._____

23. Despite the efforts of the Supervising mechanic, the elevator could not be started.   23._____

24. The U.S. Weather Bureau, weather record for the accident date was checked.   24._____

KEY (CORRECT ANSWERS)

1. D
2. A
3. B
4. D
5. D

6. D
7. C
8. A
9. A
10. D

11. A
12. B
13. D
14. B
15. C

16. C
17. A
18. A
19. B
20. C

21. D
22. C
23. C
24. B

TEST 2

DIRECTIONS: Each question consists of a sentence. Some of the sentences contain errors in English grammar or usage, punctuation, spelling, or capitalization. A sentence does not contain an error simply because it could be written in a different manner. Choose answer:
- A. If the sentence contains an error in English grammar or usage.
- B. if the sentence contains an error in punctuation.
- C. If the sentence contains an error in spelling or capitalization
- D. If the sentence does not contain any errors.

1. The severity of the sentence prescribed by contemporary statutes—including both the former and the revised New York Penal Laws—do not depend on what crime was intended by the offender.   1._____

2. It is generally recognized that two defects in the early law of attempt played a part in the birth of burglary: (1) immunity from prosecution for conduct short of the last act before completion of the crime, and (2) the relatively minor penalty imposed for an attempt (it being a common law misdemeanor) vis-à-vis the completed offense.   2._____

3. The first sentence of the statute is applicable to employees who enter their place of employment, invited guests, and all other persons who have an express or implied license or privilege to enter the premises.   3._____

4. Contemporary criminal codes in the United States generally divide burglary into various degrees, differentiating the categories according to place, time and other attendent circumstances.   4._____

5. The assignment was completed in record time but the payroll for it has not yet been prepaid.   5._____

6. The operator, on the other hand, is willing to learn me how to use the mimeograph.   6._____

7. She is the prettiest of the three sisters.   7._____

8. She doesn't know; if the mail has arrived.   8._____

9. The doorknob of the office door is broke.   9._____

10. Although the department's supply of scratch pads and stationery have diminished considerably, the allotment for our division has not been reduced.   10._____

11. You have not told us whom you wish to designate as your secretary.   11._____

12. Upon reading the minutes of the last meeting, the new proposal was taken up for consideration.   12._____

13. Before beginning the discussion, we locked the door as a precautionery measure.   13.____

14. The supervisor remarked, "Only those clerks, who perform routine work, are permitted to take a rest period."   14.____

15. Not only will this duplicating machine make accurate copies, but it will also produce a quantity of work equal to fifteen transcribing typists.   15.____

16. "Mr. Jones," said the supervisor, "we regret our inability to grant you an extention of your leave of absence."   16.____

17. Although the employees find the work monotonous and fatigueing, they rarely complain.   17.____

18. We completed the tabulation of the receipts on time despite the fact that Miss Smith our fastest operator was absent for over a week.   18.____

19. The reaction of the employees who attended the meeting, as well as the reaction of those who did not attend, indicates clearly that the schedule is satisfactory to everyone concerned.   19.____

20. Of the two employees, the one in our office is the most efficient.   20.____

21. No one can apply or even understand, the new rules and regulations.   21.____

22. A large amount of supplies were stored in the empty office.   22.____

23. If an employee is occassionally asked to work overtime, he should do so willingly.   23.____

24. It is true that the new procedures are difficult to use but, we are certain that you will learn them quickly.   24.____

25. The office manager said that he did not know who would be given a large allotment under the new plan.   25.____

KEY (CORRECT ANSWERS)

1. A
2. D
3. D
4. C
5. C

6. A
7. D
8. B
9. A
10. A

11. D
12. A
13. C
14. B
15. A

16. C
17. C
18. B
19. D
20. A

21. B
22. A
23. C
24. B
25. D

TEST 3

DIRECTIONS: Each of the following sentences may be classified MOST appropriately under one of the following categories:
    A. Faulty because of incorrect grammar
    B. Faulty because of incorrect punctuation
    C. Faulty because of incorrect capitalization
    D. Correct

Examine each sentence carefully. Then, in the space at the right, print the capital letter preceding the option which is the BEST of the four suggested above. All incorrect sentence contain but one type of error. Consider a sentence correct if it contains none of the types of errors mentioned, even though there may be other correct ways of expressing the same thought.

1. The desk, as well as the chairs, were moved out of the office.   1.____

2. The clerk whose production was greatest for the month won a day's vacation as first prize.   2.____

3. Upon entering the room, the employees were found hard at work at their desks.   3.____

4. John Smith our new employee always arrives at work on time.   4.____

5. Punish whoever is guilty of stealing the money.   5.____

6. Intelligent and persistent effort lead to success no matter what the job may be.   6.____

7. The secretary asked, "can you call again at three o'clock?"   7.____

8. He told us, that if the report was not accepted at the next meeting, it would have to be rewritten.   8.____

9. He would not have sent the letter if he had known that it would cause so much excitement.   9.____

10. We all looked forward to him coming to visit us.   10.____

11. If you find that you are unable to complete the assignment please notify me as soon as possible.   11.____

12. Every girl in the office went home on time but me; there was still some work for me to finish.   12.____

13. He wanted to know who the letter was addressed to, Mr. Brown or Mr. Smith.   13.____

14. "Mr. Jones, he said, please answer this letter as soon as possible."   14.____

15. The new clerk had an unusual accent inasmuch as he was born and educated in the south. 15._____

16. Although he is younger than her, he earns a higher salary. 16._____

17. Neither of the two administrators are going to attend the conference being held in Washington, D.C. 17._____

18. Since Miss Smith and Miss Jones have more experience than us, they have been given more responsible duties. 18._____

19. Mr. Shaw the supervisor of the stock room maintains an inventory of stationery and office supplies. 19._____

20. Inasmuch as this matter affects both you and I, we should take joint action. 20._____

21. Who do you think will be able to perform this highly technical work? 21._____

22. Of the two employees, John is considered the most competent. 22._____

23. He is not coming home on tuesday; we expect him next week. 23._____

24. Stenographers, as well as typists must be able to type rapidly and accurately. 24._____

25. Having been placed in the safe we were sure that the money would not be stolen. 25._____

KEY (CORRECT ANSWERS)

1.	A		11.	B
2.	D		12.	D
3.	A		13.	A
4.	B		14.	B
5.	D		15.	C
6.	A		16.	A
7.	C		17.	A
8.	B		18.	A
9.	D		19.	B
10.	A		20.	A

21. D
22. A
23. C
24. B
25. A

TEST 4

DIRECTIONS: Each of the following sentences consist of four sentences lettered A, B, C, and D. One of the sentences in each group contains an error in grammar or punctuation. Indicate the INCORRECT sentence in each group. *PRINT THE LETTER OF THE CORRECT ANSWER IN THE SPACE AT THE RIGHT.*

1. A. Give the message to whoever is on duty.
   B. The teacher who's pupil won first prize presented the award.
   C. Between you and me, I don't expect the program to succeed.
   D. His running to catch the bus caused the accident.

   1.____

2. A. The process, which was patented only last year is already obsolete.
   B. His interest in science (which continues to the present) led him to convert his basement into a laboratory.
   C. He described the book as "verbose, repetitious, and bombastic".
   D. Our new director will need to possess three qualities: vision, patience, and fortitude.

   2.____

3. A. The length of ladder trucks varies considerably.
   B. The probationary fireman reported to the officer to who he was assigned.
   C. The lecturer emphasized the need for we firemen to be punctual.
   D. Neither the officers nor the members of the company knew about the new procedure.

   3.____

4. A. Ham and eggs is the specialty of the house.
   B. He is one of the students who are on probation.
   C. Do you think that either one of us have a chance to be nominated for president of the class?
   D. I assume that either he was to be in charge or you were.

   4.____

5. A. Its a long road that has no turn.
   B. To run is more tiring than to walk.
   C. We have been assigned three new reports: namely, the statistical summary, the narrative summary, and the budgetary summary.
   D. Had the first payment been made in January, the second would be due in April.

   5.____

6. A. Each employer has his own responsibilities.
   B. If a person speaks correctly, they make a good impression.
   C. Every one of the operators has had her vacation.
   D. Has anybody filed his report?

   6.____

7. A. The manager, with all his salesmen, was obliged to go.
   B. Who besides them is to sign the agreement?
   C. One report without the others is incomplete.
   D. Several clerks, as well as the proprietor, was injured.

   7.____

8. A. A suspension of these activities is expected.
    B. The machine is economical because first cost and upkeep are low.
    C. A knowledge of stenography and filing are required for this position.
    D. The condition in which the goods were received shows that the packing was not done properly.

9. A. There seems to be a great many reasons for disagreement.
    B. It does not seem possible that they could have failed.
    C. Have there always been too few applicants for these positions?
    D. There is no excuse for these errors.

10. A. We shall be pleased to answer your question.
    B. Shall we plan the meeting for Saturday?
    C. I will call you promptly at seven.
    D. Can I borrow your book after you have read it?

11. A. You are as capable as I.
    B. Everyone is willing to sign but him and me.
    C. As for he and his assistant, I cannot praise them too highly.
    D. Between you and me, I think he will be dismissed.

12. A. Our competitors bid above us last week.
    B. The survey which was began last year has not yet been completed.
    C. The operators had shown that they understood their instructions.
    D. We have never ridden over worse roads.

13. A. Who did they say was responsible?
    B. Whom did you suspect?
    C. Who do you suppose it was?
    D. Whom do you mean?

14. A. Of the two propositions, this is the worse.
    B. Which report do you consider the best—the one in January or the one in July?
    C. I believe this is the most practicable of the many plans submitted.
    D. He is the youngest employee in the organization.

15. A. The firm had but three orders last week.
    B. That doesn't really seem possible.
    C. After twenty years scarcely none of the old business remains.
    D. Has he done nothing about it?

KEY (CORRECT ANSWERS)

1. B
2. A
3. C
4. C
5. A
6. B
7. D
8. C
9. A
10. D
11. C
12. B
13. A
14. B
15. C

PREPARING WRITTEN MATERIAL

PARAGRAPH REARRANGEMENT
COMMENTARY

The sentences that follow are in scrambled order. You are to rearrange them in proper order and indicate the letter choice containing the correct answer at the space at the right.

Each group of sentences in this section is actually a paragraph presented in scrambled order. Each sentence in the group has a place in that paragraph; no sentence is to be left out. You are to read each group of sentences and decide upon the best order in which to put the sentences so as to form a well-organized paragraph.

The questions in this section measure the ability to solve a problem when all the facts relevant to its solution are not given.

More specifically, certain positions of responsibility and authority require the employee to discover connection between events sometimes, apparently, unrelated. In order to do this, the employee will find it necessary to correctly infer that unspecified events have probably occurred or are likely to occur. This ability becomes especially important when action must be taken on incomplete information.

Accordingly, these questions require competitors to choose among several suggested alternatives, each of which presents a different sequential arrangement of the events. Competitors must choose the MOST logical of the suggested sequences.

In order to do so, they may be required to draw on general knowledge to infer missing concepts or events that are essential to sequencing the given events. Competitors should be careful to infer only what is essential to the sequence. The plausibility of the wrong alternatives will always require the inclusion of unlikely events or of additional chains of events which are NOT essential to sequencing the given events.

It's very important to remember that you are looking for the best of the four possible choices, and that the best choice of all may not even be one of the answers you're given to choose from.

There is no one right way to solve these problems. Many people have found it helpful to first write out the order of the sentences, as they would have arranged them, on their scrap paper before looking at the possible answers. If their optimum answer is there, this can save them some time. If it isn't, this method can still give insight into solving the problem. Others find it most helpful to just go through each of the possible choices, contrasting each as they go along. You should use whatever method feels comfortable and works for you.

While most of these types of questions are not that difficult, we've added a higher percentage of the difficult type, just to give you more practice. Usually there are only one or two questions on this section that contain such subtle distinctions that you're unable to answer confidently. And you then may find yourself stuck deciding between two possible choices, neither of which you're sure about.

EXAMINATION SECTION

TEST 1

DIRECTIONS: Each question consists of several sentences which can be arranged in a logical sequence. For each question, select the choice which places the numbered sentences in the MOST logical sequence. *PRINT THE LETTER OF THE CORRECT ANSWER IN THE SPACE AT THE RIGHT.*

1.
   I. A body was found in the woods.
   II. A man proclaimed innocence.
   III. The owner of a gun was located.
   IV. A gun was traced.
   V. The owner of a gun was questioned.
   The CORRECT answer is:
   A. IV, III, V, II, I   B. II, I, IV, III, V   C. I, IV, III, V, II
   D. I, III, V, II, IV   E. I, II, IV, III, V

   1._____

2.
   I. A man is in a hunting accident.
   II. A man fell down a flight of steps.
   III. A man lost his vision in one eye.
   IV. A man broke his leg.
   V. A man had to walk with a cane.
   The CORRECT answer is:
   A. II, IV, V, I, III   B. IV, V, I, III, II   C. III, I, IV, V, II
   D. I, III, V, II, IV   E. I, III, II, IV, V

   2._____

3.
   I. A man is offered a new job.
   II. A woman is offered a new job.
   III. A man works as a waiter.
   IV. A woman works as a waitress.
   V. A woman gives notice.
   The CORRECT answer is:
   A. IV, II, V, III, I   B. IV, II, V, I, III   C. II, IV, V, III, I
   D. III, I, IV, II, V   E. IV, III, II, V, I

   3._____

4.
   I. A train let the station late.
   II. A man was late for work.
   III. A man lost his job.
   IV. Many people complained because the train was late.
   V. There was a traffic jam.
   The CORRECT answer is:
   A. V, II, I, IV, III   B. V, I, IV, II, III   C. V, I, II, IV, III
   D. I, V, IV, II, III   E. II, I, IV, V, III

   4._____

5. I. The burden of proof as to each issue is determined before trial and remains upon the same party throughout the trial.
    II. The jury is at liberty to believe one witness' testimony as against a number of contradictory witnesses.
    III. In a civil case, the party bearing the burden of proof is required to prove his contention by a fair preponderance of the evidence.
    IV. However, it must be noted that a fair preponderance of evidence does not necessarily mean a greater number of witnesses.
    V. The burden of proof is the burden which rests upon one of the parties to an action to persuade the trier of the facts, generally the jury, that a proposition he asserts is true.
    VI. If the evidence is equally balanced, or if it leaves the jury in such doubt as to be unable to decide the controversy either way, judgment must be given against the party upon whom the burden of proof rests.
    The CORRECT answer is:
    A. III, II, V, IV, I, VI   B. I, II, VI, V, III, IV   C. III, IV, V, I, II, VI
    D. V, I, III, VI, IV, II   E. I, V, III, VI, IV, II

6. I. If a parent is without assets and is unemployed, he cannot be convicted of the crime of non-support of a child.
    II. The term *sufficient ability* has been held to mean sufficient financial ability.
    III. It does not matter if his unemployment is by choice or unavoidable circumstances.
    IV. If he fails to take any steps at all, he may be liable to prosecution for endangering the welfare of a child.
    V. Under the penal law, a parent is responsible for the support of his minor child only if the parent is of *sufficient ability*.
    VI. An indigent parent may meet his obligation by borrowing money or by seeking aid under the provisions of the Social Welfare Law.
    The CORRECT answer is:
    A. VI, I, V, III, II, IV   B. I, III, V, II, IV, VI   C. V, II, I, III, VI, IV
    D. I, VI, IV, V, II, III   E. II, V, I, III, VI, IV

7. I. Consider, for example, the case of a rabble rouser who urges a group of twenty people to go out and break the windows of a nearby factory.
    II. Therefore, the law fills the indicated gap with the crime of *inciting to riot*.
    III. A person is considered guilty of inciting to riot when he urges ten or more persons to engage in tumultuous and violent conduct of a kind likely to create public alarm.
    IV. However, if he has not obtained the cooperation of at least four people, he cannot be charged with unlawful assembly.
    V. The charge of inciting to riot was added to the law to cover types of conduct which cannot be classified as either the crime of *riot* or the crime of *unlawful assembly*.
    VI. If he acquires the acquiescence of at least four of them, he is guilty of unlawful assembly even if the project does not materialize.
    The CORRECT answer is:
    A. III, V, I, VI, IV, II   B. V, I, IV, VI, II, III   C. III, IV, I, V, II, VI
    D. V, I, IV, VI, III, II   E. V, III, I, VI, IV, II

8. I. If, however, the rebuttal evidence presents an issue of credibility, it is for the jury to determine whether the presumption has, in fact, been destroyed.
    II. Once sufficient evidence to the contrary is introduced, the presumption disappears from the trial.
    III. The effect of a presumption is to place the burden upon the adversary to come forward with evidence to rebut the presumption.
    IV. When a presumption is overcome and ceases to exist in the case, the fact or facts which gave rise to the presumption still remain.
    V. Whether a presumption has been overcome is ordinarily a question for the court.
    VI. Such information may furnish a basis for a logical inference.
    The CORRECT answer is:
    A. IV, VI, II, V, I, III   B. III, II, V, I, IV, VI   C. V, III, VI, IV, II, I
    D. V, IV, I, II, VI, III   E. II, III, V, I, IV, VI

8.____

9. I. An executive may answer a letter by writing his reply on the face of the letter itself instead of having a return letter typed.
    II. This procedure is efficient because it saves the executive's time, the typist's time, and saves office file space.
    III. Copying machines are used in small offices as well as large offices to save time and money in making brief replies to business letters.
    IV. A copy is made on a copying machine to go into the company files, while the original is mailed back to the sender.
    The CORRECT answer is:
    A. I, II, IV, III   B. I, IV, II, III   C. III, I, IV, II   D. III, IV, II, I

9.____

10. I. Most organizations favor one of the types but always include the others to a lesser degree.
    II. However, we can detect a definite trend toward greater use of symbolic control.
    III. We suggest that our local police agencies are today primarily utilizing material control.
    IV. Control can be classified into three types: physical, material, and symbolic.
    The CORRECT answer is:
    A. IV, II, III, I   B. II, I, IV, III   C. III, IV, II, I   D. IV, I, III, II

10.____

11. I. Project residents had first claim to this use, followed by surrounding neighborhood children.
    II. By contrast, recreation space within the project's interior was found to be used more often by both groups.
    III. Studies of the use of project grounds in many cities showed grounds left open for public use were neglected and unused, both by residents and by members of the surrounding community.
    IV. Project residents had clearly laid claim to the play spaces, setting up and enforcing unwritten rules for use.
    V. Each group, by experience, found their activities easily disrupted by other groups, and their claim to the use of space for recreation difficult to enforce.

11.____

The CORRECT answer is:
A. IV, V, I, II, III
B. V, II, IV, III, I
C. I, IV, III, II, V
D. III, V, II, IV, I

12. I. They do not consider the problems correctable within the existing subsidy formula and social policy of accepting all eligible applicants regardless of social behavior.
    II. A recent survey, however, indicated that tenants believe these problems correctable by local housing authorities and management within the existing financial formula.
    III. Many of the problems and complaints concerning public housing management and design have created resentment between the tenant and the landlord.
    IV. This same survey indicated that administrators and managers do not agree with the tenants.
    The CORRECT answer is:
    A. II, I, III, IV   B. I, III, IV, II   C. III, II, IV, I   D. IV, II, I, III

13. I. In single-family residences, there is usually enough distance between tenants to prevent occupants from annoying one another.
    II. For example, a certain small percentage of tenant families has one or more members addicted to alcohol.
    III. While managers believe in the right of individuals to live as they choose, the manager becomes concerned when the pattern of living jeopardizes others' rights.
    IV. Still others turn night into day, staging lusty entertainments which carry on into the hours when most tenants are trying to sleep.
    V. In apartment buildings, however, tenants live so closely together that any misbehavior can result in unpleasant living conditions.
    VI. Other families engage in violent argument.
    The CORRECT answer is:
    A. III, II, V, IV, VI, I
    B. I, V, II, VI, IV, III
    C. II, V, IV, I, III, VI
    D. IV, II, V, VI, III, I

14. I. Congress made the commitment explicit in the Housing Act of 194, establishing as a national goal the realization of a *decent home and suitable environment for every American family*.
    II. The result has been that the goal of decent home and suitable environment is still as far distant as ever for the disadvantaged urban family.
    III. In spite of this action by Congress, federal housing programs have continued to be fragmented and grossly underfunded.
    IV. The passage of the National Housing Act signaled a few federal commitment to provide housing for the nation's citizens.
    The CORRECT answer is:
    A. I, IV, III, II   B. IV, I, III, II   C. IV, I, II, III   D. II, IV, I, III

15.
I. The greater expense does not necessarily involve *exploitation*, but it is often perceived as exploitative and unfair by those who are aware of the price differences involved, but unaware of operating costs.
II. Ghetto residents believe they are *exploited* by local merchants, and evidence substantiates some of these beliefs.
III. However, stores in low-income areas were more likely to be small independents, which could not achieve the economies available to supermarket chains and were, therefore, more likely to charge higher prices, and the customers were more likely to buy smaller-sized packages which are more expensive per unit of measure.
IV. A study conducted in one city showed that distinctly higher prices were charged for goods sold in ghetto stores in other areas.
The CORRECT answer is:
  A. IV, II, I, III   B. IV, I, III, II   C. II, IV, III, I   D. II, III, IV, I

15.____

KEY (CORRECT ANSWERS)

1.	C	6.	C	11.	D
2.	E	7.	A	12.	C
3.	B	8.	B	13.	B
4.	B	9.	C	14.	B
5.	D	10.	D	15.	C

COURTROOM TERMS

A/K/A: Acronym that stands for "also known as" and introduces any alternative or assumed names or aliases of an individual. A term to indicate another name by which a person is known.

Arraignment: The bringing of a defendant before the court to answer the matters charged against him in an indictment or information. The defendant is read the charges and must respond with his plea.

Arrest: Deprivation of one's liberty by legal authority.

Bail: An amount of money set by the court to procure the release of a person from legal custody; this money is to be forfeited if the defendant fails to appear for trial.

Beyond a Reasonable Doubt: The standard of proof required for a finding of guilty in a criminal matter. Satisfied to a moral certainty. This is a higher standard of proof than that required in a civil matter (preponderance of the evidence).

Co-Defendant: Any additional defendant or respondent in the same case.

Confession: A voluntary statement made by a person charged with a crime wherein said person acknowledges his/her guilt of the offense charged and discloses participation in the act.

Controlled Dangerous Substance: That group of legally designated drugs, which, by statute, it is illegal to possess or distribute.

Criminal complaint: The initial written notice to a defendant that he/she is being charged with a public offense.

Due Process of Law: The exercise of the powers of the government with the safeguards for the protection of individual rights as set forth in the constitution, statutes, and common case law.

Felony: A crime of a more serious nature than a misdemeanor, the exact nature of which is defined by state statute and which is punishable by a term of imprisonment exceeding one year or by death.

Grand Jury: A jury of inquiry whose duty is to receive complaints and accusations in criminal cases, hear the evidence presented on the part of the state, and determine whether to indict (see "indictment" below).

Impeach: As used in the Law of Evidence, to call into question the truthfulness of a witness, by means of introducing evidence to discredit him or her.

Indictment: A written accusation presented by a grand jury after having been presented with evidence, charging that a person named therein has done some act, or has been guilty of some omission that by law is a public offense.

Miranda Warnings: The compulsory advisement of a person's rights prior to any custodial interrogation; these include: a) the right to remain silent; b) that any statement made may be used against him/her; c) the right to an attorney; d) the appointment of counsel if the accused cannot afford his or her own attorney. Unless these rights are given, any evidence obtained in an interrogation cannot be used in the individual's trial against him/her.

Misdemeanor: Offense lower than felony and generally punishable by a fine or imprisonment other than in a penitentiary.

Motion to Quash: Application to the court to set aside the complaint, indictment or subpoena due to a lack of probable cause to arrest the defendant, or in matters heard by a grand jury, due to evidence not properly presented to the grand jury.

Motion to Sever: Application to the court made when there are two defendants charged with the same crimes or who acted jointly in the commission of a crime, when their attorneys feel it would be in their best interest if they had separate trials.

Motion to Suppress Evidence: Application to the court to prevent evidence from being presented at trial when said evidence has been obtained by illegal means. It applies to physical evidence, statements made by defendant when not advised by counsel or through wiretapping, prior convictions, etc..

Parole: A conditional release from custody at the discretion of the paroling authority prior to his or her completing the prison sentence imposed. During said release the offender is required to observe conditions of this status under the supervision of a parole agency.

Plea: A defendant's formal answer in court to the charges contained in a charging document.

Guilty: A plea by the defendant in which he acknowledges guilt either of the offense charged or of a less serious offense pursuant to an agreement with the prosecuting attorney. It should be understood, however, that the court may not be obliged to recognize this.

Nolo Contendere: A plea that is admissible in some jurisdictions, in which the defendant states that he does not contest the charges against him. Also called "no contest", this plea has the same effect as a guilty plea, except that it cannot be used against the defendant in civil actions arising out of the same incident which gave rise to the criminal charges.

Not Guilty: A plea of innocence by the defendant.

Not Guilty by Reason of Insanity: A plea that is sometimes entered in conjunction with the "not guilty" plea.

Double Jeopardy: A plea entered by a defendant who has been tried for an offense wherein he asserts that he cannot be tried a second time for said offense, unless he successfully secured a new trial after an appeal, or after a motion for a new trial was granted by the trial court.

Police Report: The official report made by any police officer involved with the incident or appearing after the incident, setting forth the officer's observations and statements of parties and witnesses. It can be used as evidence in a trial.

Pre-Trial Intervention: Utilized in some states when a defendant is accused of a first offense, to divert the defendant from the criminal justice system.

Probation: To allow a person convicted of a minor offense to go at large, under a suspension of sentence, during good behavior, and generally under the supervision of a probation officer.

Prosecutor: The attorney who prosecutes defendants for crimes, in the name of the government.

Search Warrant: A written order, issued by the court, directing the police to search a specified location for particular personal property (stolen or illegally possessed).

Speedy Trial: Mandate by the government that all criminal trials must take place within a specified time after arrest.

Writ of Habeas Corpus: A mandate issued from a court requiring that an individual be brought before the court.

GLOSSARY OF LEGAL TERMS

TABLE OF CONTENTS

	Page
Action ... Affiant	1
Affidavit ... At Bar	2
At Issue ... Burden of Proof	3
Business ... Commute	4
Complainant ... Conviction	5
Cooperative ... Demur (v.)	6
Demurrage ... Endorsement	7
Enjoin ... Facsimile	8
Factor ... Guilty	9
Habeas Corpus ... Incumbrance	10
Indemnify ... Laches	11
Landlord and Tenant ... Malice	12
Mandamus ... Obiter Dictum	13
Object (v.) ... Perjury	14
Perpetuity ... Proclamation	15
Proffered Evidence ... Referee	16
Referendum ... Stare Decisis	17
State ... Term	18
Testamentary ... Warrant (Warranty) (v.)	19
Warrant (n.) ... Zoning	20

GLOSSARY OF LEGAL TERMS

A

ACTION - "Action" includes a civil action and a criminal action.
A FORTIORI - A term meaning you can reason one thing from the existence of certain facts.
A POSTERIORI - From what goes after; from effect to cause.
A PRIORI - From what goes before; from cause to effect.
AB INITIO - From the beginning.
ABATE - To diminish or put an end to.
ABET - To encourage the commission of a crime.
ABEYANCE - Suspension, temporary suppression.
ABIDE - To accept the consequences of.
ABJURE - To renounce; give up.
ABRIDGE - To reduce; contract; diminish.
ABROGATE - To annul, repeal, or destroy.
ABSCOND - To hide or absent oneself to avoid legal action.
ABSTRACT - A summary.
ABUT - To border on, to touch.
ACCESS - Approach; in real property law it means the right of the owner of property to the use of the highway or road next to his land, without obstruction by intervening property owners.
ACCESSORY - In criminal law, it means the person who contributes or aids in the commission of a crime.
ACCOMMODATED PARTY - One to whom credit is extended on the strength of another person signing a commercial paper.
ACCOMMODATION PAPER - A commercial paper to which the accommodating party has put his name.
ACCOMPLICE - In criminal law, it means a person who together with the principal offender commits a crime.
ACCORD - An agreement to accept something different or less than that to which one is entitled, which extinguishes the entire obligation.
ACCOUNT - A statement of mutual demands in the nature of debt and credit between parties.
ACCRETION - The act of adding to a thing; in real property law, it means gradual accumulation of land by natural causes.
ACCRUE - To grow to; to be added to.
ACKNOWLEDGMENT - The act of going before an official authorized to take acknowledgments, and acknowledging an act as one's own.
ACQUIESCENCE - A silent appearance of consent.
ACQUIT - To legally determine the innocence of one charged with a crime.
AD INFINITUM - Indefinitely.
AD LITEM - For the suit.
AD VALOREM - According to value.
ADJECTIVE LAW - Rules of procedure.
ADJUDICATION - The judgment given in a case.
ADMIRALTY - Court having jurisdiction over maritime cases.
ADULT - Sixteen years old or over (in criminal law).
ADVANCE - In commercial law, it means to pay money or render other value before it is due.
ADVERSE - Opposed; contrary.
ADVOCATE - (v.) To speak in favor of;
          (n.) One who assists, defends, or pleads for another.
AFFIANT - A person who makes and signs an affidavit.

AFFIDAVIT - A written and sworn to declaration of facts, voluntarily made.
AFFINITY- The relationship between persons through marriage with the kindred of each other; distinguished from consanguinity, which is the relationship by blood.
AFFIRM - To ratify; also when an appellate court affirms a judgment, decree, or order, it means that it is valid and right and must stand as rendered in the lower court.
AFOREMENTIONED; AFORESAID - Before or already said.
AGENT - One who represents and acts for another.
AID AND COMFORT - To help; encourage.
ALIAS - A name not one's true name.
ALIBI - A claim of not being present at a certain place at a certain time.
ALLEGE - To assert.
ALLOTMENT - A share or portion.
AMBIGUITY - Uncertainty; capable of being understood in more than one way.
AMENDMENT - Any language made or proposed as a change in some principal writing.
AMICUS CURIAE - A friend of the court; one who has an interest in a case, although not a party in the case, who volunteers advice upon matters of law to the judge. For example, a brief amicus curiae.
AMORTIZATION - To provide for a gradual extinction of (a future obligation) in advance of maturity, especially, by periodical contributions to a sinking fund which will be adequate to discharge a debt or make a replacement when it becomes necessary.
ANCILLARY - Aiding, auxiliary.
ANNOTATION - A note added by way of comment or explanation.
ANSWER - A written statement made by a defendant setting forth the grounds of his defense.
ANTE - Before.
ANTE MORTEM - Before death.
APPEAL - The removal of a case from a lower court to one of superior jurisdiction for the purpose of obtaining a review.
APPEARANCE - Coming into court as a party to a suit.
APPELLANT - The party who takes an appeal from one court or jurisdiction to another (appellate) court for review.
APPELLEE - The party against whom an appeal is taken.
APPROPRIATE - To make a thing one's own.
APPROPRIATION - Prescribing the destination of a thing; the act of the legislature designating a particular fund, to be applied to some object of government expenditure.
APPURTENANT - Belonging to; accessory or incident to.
ARBITER - One who decides a dispute; a referee.
ARBITRARY - Unreasoned; not governed by any fixed rules or standard.
ARGUENDO - By way of argument.
ARRAIGN - To call the prisoner before the court to answer to a charge.
ASSENT - A declaration of willingness to do something in compliance with a request.
ASSERT - Declare.
ASSESS - To fix the rate or amount.
ASSIGN - To transfer; to appoint; to select for a particular purpose.
ASSIGNEE - One who receives an assignment.
ASSIGNOR - One who makes an assignment.
AT BAR - Before the court.

AT ISSUE - When parties in an action come to a point where one asserts something and the other denies it.
ATTACH - Seize property by court order and sometimes arrest a person.
ATTEST - To witness a will, etc.; act of attestation.
AVERMENT - A positive statement of facts.

B

BAIL - To obtain the release of a person from legal custody by giving security and promising that he shall appear in court; to deliver (goods, etc.) in trust to a person for a special purpose.
BAILEE - One to whom personal property is delivered under a contract of bailment.
BAILMENT - Delivery of personal property to another to be held for a certain purpose and to be returned when the purpose is accomplished.
BAILOR - The party who delivers goods to another, under a contract of bailment.
BANC (OR BANK) - Bench; the place where a court sits permanently or regularly; also the assembly of all the judges of a court.
BANKRUPT - An insolvent person, technically, one declared to be bankrupt after a bankruptcy proceeding.
BAR - The legal profession.
BARRATRY - Exciting groundless judicial proceedings.
BARTER - A contract by which parties exchange goods for other goods.
BATTERY - Illegal interfering with another's person.
BEARER - In commercial law, it means the person in possession of a commercial paper which is payable to the bearer.
BENCH - The court itself or the judge.
BENEFICIARY - A person benefiting under a will, trust, or agreement.
BEST EVIDENCE RULE, THE - Except as otherwise provided by statute, no evidence other than the writing itself is admissible to prove the content of a writing. This section shall be known and may be cited as the best evidence rule.
BEQUEST - A gift of personal property under a will.
BILL - A formal written statement of complaint to a court of justice; also, a draft of an act of the legislature before it becomes a law; also, accounts for goods sold, services rendered, or work done.
BONA FIDE - In or with good faith; honestly.
BOND - An instrument by which the maker promises to pay a sum of money to another, usually providing that upon performances of a certain condition the obligation shall be void.
BOYCOTT - A plan to prevent the carrying on of a business by wrongful means.
BREACH - The breaking or violating of a law, or the failure to carry out a duty.
BRIEF - A written document, prepared by a lawyer to serve as the basis of an argument upon a case in court, usually an appellate court.
BURDEN OF PRODUCING EVIDENCE - The obligation of a party to introduce evidence sufficient to avoid a ruling against him on the issue.
BURDEN OF PROOF - The obligation of a party to establish by evidence a requisite degree of belief concerning a fact in the mind of the trier of fact or the court. The burden of proof may require a party to raise a reasonable doubt concerning the existence of nonexistence of a fact or that he establish the existence or nonexistence of a fact by a preponderance of the evidence, by clear and convincing proof, or by proof beyond a reasonable doubt.

    Except as otherwise provided by law, the burden of proof requires proof by a preponderance of the evidence.

BUSINESS, A - Shall include every kind of business, profession, occupation, calling or operation of institutions, whether carried on for profit or not.

BY-LAWS - Regulations, ordinances, or rules enacted by a corporation, association, etc., for its own government.

C

CANON - A doctrine; also, a law or rule, of a church or association in particular.

CAPIAS - An order to arrest.

CAPTION - In a pleading, deposition or other paper connected with a case in court, it is the heading or introductory clause which shows the names of the parties, name of the court, number of the case on the docket or calendar, etc.

CARRIER - A person or corporation undertaking to transport persons or property.

CASE - A general term for an action, cause, suit, or controversy before a judicial body.

CAUSE - A suit, litigation or action before a court.

CAVEAT EMPTOR - Let the buyer beware. This term expresses the rule that the purchaser of an article must examine, judge, and test it for himself, being bound to discover any obvious defects or imperfections.

CERTIFICATE - A written representation that some legal formality has been complied with.

CERTIORARI - To be informed of; the name of a writ issued by a superior court directing the lower court to send up to the former the record and proceedings of a case.

CHANGE OF VENUE - To remove place of trial from one place to another.

CHARGE - An obligation or duty; a formal complaint; an instruction of the court to the jury upon a case.

CHARTER - (n.) The authority by virtue of which an organized body acts;
(v.) in mercantile law, it means to hire or lease a vehicle or vessel for transportation.

CHATTEL - An article of personal property.

CHATTEL MORTGAGE - A mortgage on personal property.

CIRCUIT - A division of the country, for the administration of justice; a geographical area served by a court.

CITATION - The act of the court by which a person is summoned or cited; also, a reference to legal authority.

CIVIL (ACTIONS)- It indicates the private rights and remedies of individuals in contrast to the word "criminal" (actions) which relates to prosecution for violation of laws.

CLAIM (n.) - Any demand held or asserted as of right.

CODICIL - An addition to a will.

CODIFY - To arrange the laws of a country into a code.

COGNIZANCE - Notice or knowledge.

COLLATERAL - By the side; accompanying; an article or thing given to secure performance of a promise.

COMITY - Courtesy; the practice by which one court follows the decision of another court on the same question.

COMMIT - To perform, as an act; to perpetrate, as a crime; to send a person to prison.

COMMON LAW - As distinguished from law created by the enactment of the legislature (called statutory law), it relates to those principles and rules of action which derive their authority solely from usages and customs of immemorial antiquity, particularly with reference to the ancient unwritten law of England. The written pronouncements of the common law are found in court decisions.

COMMUTE - Change punishment to one less severe.

COMPLAINANT - One who applies to the court for legal redress.
COMPLAINT - The pleading of a plaintiff in a civil action; or a charge that a person has committed a specified offense.
COMPROMISE - An arrangement for settling a dispute by agreement.
CONCUR - To agree, consent.
CONCURRENT - Running together, at the same time.
CONDEMNATION - Taking private property for public use on payment therefor.
CONDITION - Mode or state of being; a qualification or restriction.
CONDUCT - Active and passive behavior; both verbal and nonverbal.
CONFESSION - Voluntary statement of guilt of crime.
CONFIDENTIAL COMMUNICATION BETWEEN CLIENT AND LAWYER - Information transmitted between a client and his lawyer in the course of that relationship and in confidence by a means which, so far as the client is aware, discloses the information to no third persons other than those who are present to further the interest of the client in the consultation or those to whom disclosure is reasonably necessary for the transmission of the information or the accomplishment of the purpose for which the lawyer is consulted, and includes a legal opinion formed and the advice given by the lawyer in the course of that relationship.
CONFRONTATION - Witness testifying in presence of defendant.
CONSANGUINITY - Blood relationship.
CONSIGN - To give in charge; commit; entrust; to send or transmit goods to a merchant, factor, or agent for sale.
CONSIGNEE - One to whom a consignment is made.
CONSIGNOR - One who sends or makes a consignment.
CONSPIRACY - In criminal law, it means an agreement between two or more persons to commit an unlawful act.
CONSPIRATORS - Persons involved in a conspiracy.
CONSTITUTION - The fundamental law of a nation or state.
CONSTRUCTION OF GENDERS - The masculine gender includes the feminine and neuter.
CONSTRUCTION OF SINGULAR AND PLURAL - The singular number includes the plural; and the plural, the singular.
CONSTRUCTION OF TENSES - The present tense includes the past and future tenses; and the future, the present.
CONSTRUCTIVE - An act or condition assumed from other parts or conditions.
CONSTRUE - To ascertain the meaning of language.
CONSUMMATE - To complete.
CONTIGUOUS - Adjoining; touching; bounded by.
CONTINGENT - Possible, but not assured; dependent upon some condition.
CONTINUANCE - The adjournment or postponement of an action pending in a court.
CONTRA - Against, opposed to; contrary.
CONTRACT - An agreement between two or more persons to do or not to do a particular thing.
CONTROVERT - To dispute, deny.
CONVERSION - Dealing with the personal property of another as if it were one's own, without right.
CONVEYANCE - An instrument transferring title to land.
CONVICTION - Generally, the result of a criminal trial which ends in a judgment or sentence that the defendant is guilty as charged.

COOPERATIVE - A cooperative is a voluntary organization of persons with a common interest, formed and operated along democratic lines for the purpose of supplying services at cost to its members and other patrons, who contribute both capital and business.

CORPUS DELICTI - The body of a crime; the crime itself.

CORROBORATE - To strengthen; to add weight by additional evidence.

COUNTERCLAIM - A claim presented by a defendant in opposition to or deduction from the claim of the plaintiff.

COUNTY - Political subdivision of a state.

COVENANT - Agreement.

CREDIBLE - Worthy of belief.

CREDITOR - A person to whom a debt is owing by another person, called the "debtor."

CRIMINAL ACTION - Includes criminal proceedings.

CRIMINAL INFORMATION - Same as complaint.

CRITERION (sing.)

CRITERIA (plural) - A means or tests for judging; a standard or standards.

CROSS-EXAMINATION - Examination of a witness by a party other than the direct examiner upon a matter that is within the scope of the direct examination of the witness.

CULPABLE - Blamable.

CY-PRES - As near as (possible). The rule of *cy-pres* is a rule for the construction of instruments in equity by which the intention of the party is carried out *as near as may be*, when it would be impossible or illegal to give it literal effect.

D

DAMAGES - A monetary compensation, which may be recovered in the courts by any person who has suffered loss, or injury, whether to his person, property or rights through the unlawful act or omission or negligence of another.

DECLARANT - A person who makes a statement.

DE FACTO - In fact; actually but without legal authority.

DE JURE - Of right; legitimate; lawful.

DE MINIMIS - Very small or trifling.

DE NOVO - Anew; afresh; a second time.

DEBT - A specified sum of money owing to one person from another, including not only the obligation of the debtor to pay, but the right of the creditor to receive and enforce payment.

DECEDENT - A dead person.

DECISION - A judgment or decree pronounced by a court in determination of a case.

DECREE - An order of the court, determining the rights of all parties to a suit.

DEED - A writing containing a contract sealed and delivered; particularly to convey real property.

DEFALCATION - Misappropriation of funds.

DEFAMATION - Injuring one's reputation by false statements.

DEFAULT - The failure to fulfill a duty, observe a promise, discharge an obligation, or perform an agreement.

DEFENDANT - The person defending or denying; the party against whom relief or recovery is sought in an action or suit.

DEFRAUD - To practice fraud; to cheat or trick.

DELEGATE (v.)- To entrust to the care or management of another.

DELICTUS - A crime.

DEMUR (v.) - To dispute the sufficiency in law of the pleading of the other side.

DEMURRAGE - In maritime law, it means, the sum fixed or allowed as remuneration to the owners of a ship for the detention of their vessel beyond the number of days allowed for loading and unloading or for sailing; also used in railroad terminology.

DENIAL - A form of pleading; refusing to admit the truth of a statement, charge, etc.

DEPONENT - One who gives testimony under oath reduced to writing.

DEPOSITION - Testimony given under oath outside of court for use in court or for the purpose of obtaining information in preparation for trial of a case.

DETERIORATION - A degeneration such as from decay, corrosion or disintegration.

DETRIMENT - Any loss or harm to person or property.

DEVIATION - A turning aside.

DEVISE - A gift of real property by the last will and testament of the donor.

DICTUM (sing.)
DICTA (plural) - Any statements made by the court in an opinion concerning some rule of law not necessarily involved nor essential to the determination of the case.

DIRECT EVIDENCE - Evidence that directly proves a fact, without an inference or presumption, and which in itself if true, conclusively establishes that fact.

DIRECT EXAMINATION - The first examination of a witness upon a matter that is not within the scope of a previous examination of the witness.

DISAFFIRM - To repudiate.

DISMISS - In an action or suit, it means to dispose of the case without any further consideration or hearing.

DISSENT - To denote disagreement of one or more judges of a court with the decision passed by the majority upon a case before them.

DOCKET (n.) - A formal record, entered in brief, of the proceedings in a court.

DOCTRINE - A rule, principle, theory of law.

DOMICILE - That place where a man has his true, fixed and permanent home to which whenever he is absent he has the intention of returning.

DRAFT (n.) - A commercial paper ordering payment of money drawn by one person on another.

DRAWEE - The person who is requested to pay the money.

DRAWER - The person who draws the commercial paper and addresses it to the drawee.

DUPLICATE - A counterpart produced by the same impression as the original enlargements and miniatures, or by mechanical or electronic re-recording, or by chemical reproduction, or by other equivalent technique which accurately reproduces the original.

DURESS - Use of force to compel performance or non-performance of an act.

E

EASEMENT - A liberty, privilege, or advantage without profit, in the lands of another.

EGRESS - Act or right of going out or leaving; emergence.

EIUSDEM GENERIS - Of the same kind, class or nature. A rule used in the construction of language in a legal document.

EMBEZZLEMENT - To steal; to appropriate fraudulently to one's own use property entrusted to one's care.

EMBRACERY - Unlawful attempt to influence jurors, etc., but not by offering value.

EMINENT DOMAIN - The right of a state to take private property for public use.

ENACT - To make into a law.

ENDORSEMENT - Act of writing one's name on the back of a note, bill or similar written instrument.

ENJOIN - To require a person, by writ of injunction from a court of equity, to perform or to abstain or desist from some act.
ENTIRETY - The whole; that which the law considers as one whole, and not capable of being divided into parts.
ENTRAPMENT - Inducing one to commit a crime so as to arrest him.
ENUMERATED - Mentioned specifically; designated.
ENURE - To operate or take effect.
EQUITY - In its broadest sense, this term denotes the spirit and the habit of fairness, justness, and right dealing which regulate the conduct of men.
ERROR - A mistake of law, or the false or irregular application of law as will nullify the judicial proceedings.
ESCROW - A deed, bond or other written engagement, delivered to a third person, to be delivered by him only upon the performance or fulfillment of some condition.
ESTATE - The interest which any one has in lands, or in any other subject of property.
ESTOP - To stop, bar, or impede.
ESTOPPEL - A rule of law which prevents a man from alleging or denying a fact, because of his own previous act.
ET AL. (alii) - And others.
ET SEQ. (sequential) - And the following.
ET UX. (uxor) - And wife.
EVIDENCE - Testimony, writings, material objects, or other things presented to the senses that are offered to prove the existence or non-existence of a fact.
 Means from which inferences may be drawn as a basis of proof in duly constituted judicial or fact finding tribunals, and includes testimony in the form of opinion and hearsay.
EX CONTRACTU
EX DELICTO - In law, rights and causes of action are divided into two classes, those arising *ex contractu* (from a contract) and those arising *ex delicto* (from a delict or tort).
EX OFFICIO - From office; by virtue of the office.
EX PARTE - On one side only; by or for one.
EX POST FACTO - After the fact.
EX POST FACTO LAW - A law passed after an act was done which retroactively makes such act a crime.
EX REL. (relations) - Upon relation or information.
EXCEPTION - An objection upon a matter of law to a decision made, either before or after judgment by a court.
EXECUTOR (male)
EXECUTRIX (female) - A person who has been appointed by will to execute the will.
EXECUTORY - That which is yet to be executed or performed.
EXEMPT - To release from some liability to which others are subject.
EXONERATION - The removal of a burden, charge or duty.
EXTRADITION - Surrender of a fugitive from one nation to another.

F

F.A.S.- "Free alongside ship"; delivery at dock for ship named.
F.O.B.- "Free on board"; seller will deliver to car, truck, vessel, or other conveyance by which goods are to be transported, without expense or risk of loss to the buyer or consignee.
FABRICATE - To construct; to invent a false story.
FACSIMILE - An exact or accurate copy of an original instrument.

FACTOR - A commercial agent.
FEASANCE - The doing of an act.
FELONIOUS - Criminal, malicious.
FELONY - Generally, a criminal offense that may be punished by death or imprisonment for more than one year as differentiated from a misdemeanor.
FEME SOLE - A single woman.
FIDUCIARY - A person who is invested with rights and powers to be exercised for the benefit of another person.
FIERI FACIAS - A writ of execution commanding the sheriff to levy and collect the amount of a judgment from the goods and chattels of the judgment debtor.
FINDING OF FACT - Determination from proof or judicial notice of the existence of a fact. A ruling implies a supporting finding of fact; no separate or formal finding is required unless required by a statute of this state.
FISCAL - Relating to accounts or the management of revenue.
FORECLOSURE (sale) - A sale of mortgaged property to obtain satisfaction of the mortgage out of the sale proceeds.
FORFEITURE - A penalty, a fine.
FORGERY - Fabricating or producing falsely, counterfeited.
FORTUITOUS - Accidental.
FORUM - A court of justice; a place of jurisdiction.
FRAUD - Deception; trickery.
FREEHOLDER - One who owns real property.
FUNGIBLE - Of such kind or nature that one specimen or part may be used in the place of another.

G

GARNISHEE - Person garnished.
GARNISHMENT - A legal process to reach the money or effects of a defendant, in the possession or control of a third person.
GRAND JURY - Not less than 16, not more than 23 citizens of a county sworn to inquire into crimes committed or triable in the county.
GRANT - To agree to; convey, especially real property.
GRANTEE - The person to whom a grant is made.
GRANTOR - The person by whom a grant is made.
GRATUITOUS - Given without a return, compensation or consideration.
GRAVAMEN - The grievance complained of or the substantial cause of a criminal action.
GUARANTY (n.) - A promise to answer for the payment of some debt, or the performance of some duty, in case of the failure of another person, who, in the first instance, is liable for such payment or performance.
GUARDIAN - The person, committee, or other representative authorized by law to protect the person or estate or both of an incompetent (or of a *sui juris* person having a guardian) and to act for him in matters affecting his person or property or both. An incompetent is a person under disability imposed by law.
GUILTY - Establishment of the fact that one has committed a breach of conduct; especially, a violation of law.

H

HABEAS CORPUS - You have the body; the name given to a variety of writs, having for their object to bring a party before a court or judge for decision as to whether such person is being lawfully held prisoner.
HABENDUM - In conveyancing; it is the clause in a deed conveying land which defines the extent of ownership to be held by the grantee.
HEARING - A proceeding whereby the arguments of the interested parties are heared.
HEARSAY - A type of testimony given by a witness who relates, not what he knows personally, but what others have told hi, or what he has heard said by others.
HEARSAY RULE, THE - (a) "Hearsay evidence" is evidence of a statement that was made other than by a witness while testifying at the hearing and that is offered to prove the truth of the matter stated; (b) Except as provided by law, hearsay evidence is inadmissible; (c) This section shall be known and may be cited as the hearsay rule.
HEIR - Generally, one who inherits property, real or personal.
HOLDER OF THE PRIVILEGE - (a) The client when he has no guardian or conservator; (b) A guardian or conservator of the client when the client has a guardian or conservator; (c) The personal representative of the client if the client is dead; (d) A successor, assign, trustee in dissolution, or any similar representative of a firm, association, organization, partnership, business trust, corporation, or public entity that is no longer in existence.
HUNG JURY - One so divided that they can't agree on a verdict.
HUSBAND-WIFE PRIVILEGE - An accused in a criminal proceeding has a privilege to prevent his spouse from testifying against him.
HYPOTHECATE - To pledge a thing without delivering it to the pledgee.
HYPOTHESIS - A supposition, assumption, or toehry.

I

I.E. (id est) - That is.
IB., OR IBID.(ibidem) - In the same place; used to refer to a legal reference previously cited to avoid repeating the entire citation.
ILLICIT - Prohibited; unlawful.
ILLUSORY - Deceiving by false appearance.
IMMUNITY - Exemption.
IMPEACH - To accuse, to dispute.
IMPEDIMENTS - Disabilities, or hindrances.
IMPLEAD - To sue or prosecute by due course of law.
IMPUTED - Attributed or charged to.
IN LOCO PARENTIS - In place of parent, a guardian.
IN TOTO - In the whole; completely.
INCHOATE - Imperfect; unfinished.
INCOMMUNICADO - Denial of the right of a prisoner to communicate with friends or relatives.
INCOMPETENT - One who is incapable of caring for his own affairs because he is mentally deficient or undeveloped.
INCRIMINATION - A matter will incriminate a person if it constitutes, or forms an essential part of, or, taken in connection with other matters disclosed, is a basis for a reasonable inference of such a violation of the laws of this State as to subject him to liability to punishment therefor, unless he has become for any reason permanently immune from punishment for such violation.
INCUMBRANCE - Generally a claim, lien, charge or liability attached to and binding real property.

INDEMNIFY - To secure against loss or damage; also, to make reimbursement to one for a loss already incurred by him.
INDEMNITY - An agreement to reimburse another person in case of an anticipated loss falling upon him.
INDICIA - Signs; indications.
INDICTMENT - An accusation in writing found and presented by a grand jury charging that a person has committed a crime.
INDORSE - To write a name on the back of a legal paper or document, generally, a negotiable instrument
INDUCEMENT - Cause or reason why a thing is done or that which incites the person to do the act or commit a crime; the motive for the criminal act.
INFANT - In civil cases one under 21 years of age.
INFORMATION - A formal accusation of crime made by a prosecuting attorney.
INFRA - Below, under; this word occurring by itself in a publication refers the reader to a future part of the publication.
INGRESS - The act of going into.
INJUNCTION - A writ or order by the court requiring a person, generally, to do or to refrain from doing an act.
INSOLVENT - The condition of a person who is unable to pay his debts.
INSTRUCTION - A direction given by the judge to the jury concerning the law of the case.
INTERIM - In the meantime; time intervening.
INTERLOCUTORY - Temporary, not final; something intervening between the commencement and the end of a suit which decides some point or matter, but is not a final decision of the whole controversy.
INTERROGATORIES - A series of formal written questions used in the examination of a party or a witness usually prior to a trial.
INTESTATE - A person who dies without a will.
INURE - To result, to take effect.
IPSO FACTO - By the fact iself; by the mere fact.
ISSUE (n.) The disputed point or question in a case,

J

JEOPARDY - Danger, hazard, peril.
JOINDER - Joining; uniting with another person in some legal steps or proceeding.
JOINT - United; combined.
JUDGE - Member or members or representative or representatives of a court conducting a trial or hearing at which evidence is introduced.
JUDGMENT - The official decision of a court of justice.
JUDICIAL OR JUDICIARY - Relating to or connected with the administration of justice.
JURAT - The clause written at the foot of an affidavit, stating when, where and before whom such affidavit was sworn.
JURISDICTION - The authority to hear and determine controversies between parties.
JURISPRUDENCE - The philosophy of law.
JURY - A body of persons legally selected to inquire into any matter of fact, and to render their verdict according to the evidence.

L

LACHES - The failure to diligently assert a right, which results in a refusal to allow relief.

LANDLORD AND TENANT - A phrase used to denote the legal relation existing between the owner and occupant of real estate.

LARCENY - Stealing personal property belonging to another.

LATENT - Hidden; that which does not appear on the face of a thing.

LAW - Includes constitutional, statutory, and decisional law.

LAWYER-CLIENT PRIVILEGE - (1) A "client" is a person, public officer, or corporation, association, or other organization or entity, either public or private, who is rendered professional legal services by a lawyer, or who consults a lawyer with a view to obtaining professional legal services from him; (2) A "lawyer" is a person authorized, or reasonably believed by the client to be authorized, to practice law in any state or nation; (3) A "representative of the lawyer" is one employed to assist the lawyer in the rendition of professional legal services; (4) A communication is "confidential" if not intended to be disclosed to third persons other than those to whom disclosure is in furtherance of the rendition of professional legal services to the client or those reasonably necessary for the transmission of the communication.

General rule of privilege - A client has a privilege to refuse to disclose and to prevent any other person from disclosing confidential communications made for the purpose of facilitating the rendition of professional legal services to the client, (1) between himself or his representative and his lawyer or his lawyer's representative, or (2) between his lawyer and the lawyer's representative, or (3) by him or his lawyer to a lawyer representing another in a matter of common interest, or (4) between representatives of the client or between the client and a representative of the client, or (5) between lawyers representing the client.

LEADING QUESTION - Question that suggests to the witness the answer that the examining party desires.

LEASE - A contract by which one conveys real estate for a limited time usually for a specified rent; personal property also may be leased.

LEGISLATION - The act of enacting laws.

LEGITIMATE - Lawful.

LESSEE - One to whom a lease is given.

LESSOR - One who grants a lease

LEVY - A collecting or exacting by authority.

LIABLE - Responsible; bound or obligated in law or equity.

LIBEL (v.) - To defame or injure a person's reputation by a published writing.

(n.) - The initial pleading on the part of the plaintiff in an admiralty proceeding.

LIEN - A hold or claim which one person has upon the property of another as a security for some debt or charge.

LIQUIDATED - Fixed; settled.

LIS PENDENS - A pending civil or criminal action.

LITERAL - According to the language.

LITIGANT - A party to a lawsuit.

LITATION - A judicial controversy.

LOCUS - A place.

LOCUS DELICTI - Place of the crime.

LOCUS POENITENTIAE - The abandoning or giving up of one's intention to commit some crime before it is fully completed or abandoning a conspiracy before its purpose is accomplished.

M

MALFEASANCE - To do a wrongful act.

MALICE - The doing of a wrongful act Intentionally without just cause or excuse.

MANDAMUS - The name of a writ issued by a court to enforce the performance of some public duty.
MANDATORY (adj.) Containing a command.
MARITIME - Pertaining to the sea or to commerce thereon.
MARSHALING - Arranging or disposing of in order.
MAXIM - An established principle or proposition.
MINISTERIAL - That which involves obedience to instruction, but demands no special discretion, judgment or skill.
MISAPPROPRIATE - Dealing fraudulently with property entrusted to one.
MISDEMEANOR - A crime less than a felony and punishable by a fine or imprisonment for less than one year.
MISFEASANCE - Improper performance of a lawful act.
MISREPRESENTATION - An untrue representation of facts.
MITIGATE - To make or become less severe, harsh.
MITTIMUS - A warrant of commitment to prison.
MOOT (adj.) Unsettled, undecided, not necessary to be decided.
MORTGAGE - A conveyance of property upon condition, as security for the payment of a debt or the performance of a duty, and to become void upon payment or performance according to the stipulated terms.
MORTGAGEE - A person to whom property is mortgaged.
MORTGAGOR - One who gives a mortgage.
MOTION - In legal proceedings, a "motion" is an application, either written or oral, addressed to the court by a party to an action or a suit requesting the ruling of the court on a matter of law.
MUTUALITY - Reciprocation.

N

NEGLIGENCE - The failure to exercise that degree of care which an ordinarily prudent person would exercise under like circumstances.
NEGOTIABLE (instrument) - Any instrument obligating the payment of money which is transferable from one person to another by endorsement and delivery or by delivery only.
NEGOTIATE - To transact business; to transfer a negotiable instrument; to seek agreement for the amicable disposition of a controversy or case.
NOLLE PROSEQUI - A formal entry upon the record, by the plaintiff in a civil suit or the prosecuting officer in a criminal action, by which he declares that he "will no further prosecute" the case.
NOLO CONTENDERE - The name of a plea in a criminal action, having the same effect as a plea of guilty; but not constituting a direct admission of guilt.
NOMINAL - Not real or substantial.
NOMINAL DAMAGES - Award of a trifling sum where no substantial injury is proved to have been sustained.
NONFEASANCE - Neglect of duty.
NOVATION - The substitution of a new debt or obligation for an existing one.
NUNC PRO TUNC - A phrase applied to acts allowed to be done after the time when they should be done, with a retroactive effect.("Now for then.")

O

OATH - Oath includes affirmation or declaration under penalty of perjury.
OBITER DICTUM - Opinion expressed by a court on a matter not essentially involved in a case and hence not a decision; also called dicta, if plural.

OBJECT (v.) - To oppose as improper or illegal and referring the question of its propriety or legality to the court.
OBLIGATION - A legal duty, by which a person is bound to do or not to do a certain thing.
OBLIGEE - The person to whom an obligation is owed.
OBLIGOR - The person who is to perform the obligation.
OFFER (v.) - To present for acceptance or rejection.
 (n.) - A proposal to do a thing, usually a proposal to make a contract.
OFFICIAL INFORMATION - Information within the custody or control of a department or agency of the government the disclosure of which is shown to be contrary to the public interest.
OFFSET - A deduction.
ONUS PROBANDI - Burden of proof.
OPINION - The statement by a judge of the decision reached in a case, giving the law as applied to the case and giving reasons for the judgment; also a belief or view.
OPTION - The exercise of the power of choice; also a privilege existing in one person, for which he has paid money, which gives him the right to buy or sell real or personal property at a given price within a specified time.
ORDER - A rule or regulation; every direction of a court or judge made or entered in writing but not including a judgment.
ORDINANCE - Generally, a rule established by authority; also commonly used to designate the legislative acts of a municipal corporation.
ORIGINAL - Writing or recording itself or any counterpart intended to have the same effect by a person executing or issuing it. An "original" of a photograph includes the negative or any print therefrom. If data are stored in a computer or similar device, any printout or other output readable by sight, shown to reflect the data accurately, is an "original."
OVERT - Open, manifest.

P

PANEL - A group of jurors selected to serve during a term of the court.
PARENS PATRIAE - Sovereign power of a state to protect or be a guardian over children and incompetents.
PAROL - Oral or verbal.
PAROLE - To release one in prison before the expiration of his sentence, conditionally.
PARITY - Equality in purchasing power between the farmer and other segments of the economy.
PARTITION - A legal division of real or personal property between one or more owners.
PARTNERSHIP - An association of two or more persons to carry on as co-owners a business for profit.
PATENT (adj.) - Evident.
 (n.) - A grant of some privilege, property, or authority, made by the government or sovereign of a country to one or more individuals.
PECULATION - Stealing.
PECUNIARY - Monetary.
PENULTIMATE - Next to the last.
PER CURIAM - A phrase used in the report of a decision to distinguish an opinion of the whole court from an opinion written by any one judge.
PER SE - In itself; taken alone.
PERCEIVE - To acquire knowledge through one's senses.
PEREMPTORY - Imperative; absolute.
PERJURY - To lie or state falsely under oath.

PERPETUITY - Perpetual existence; also the quality or condition of an estate limited so that it will not take effect or vest within the period fixed by law.
PERSON - Includes a natural person, firm, association, organization, partnership, business trust, corporation, or public entity.
PERSONAL PROPERTY - Includes money, goods, chattels, things in action, and evidences of debt.
PERSONALTY - Short term for personal property.
PETITION - An application in writing for an order of the court, stating the circumstances upon which it is founded and requesting any order or other relief from a court.
PLAINTIFF - A person who brings a court action.
PLEA - A pleading in a suit or action.
PLEADINGS - Formal allegations made by the parties of their respective claims and defenses, for the judgment of the court.
PLEDGE - A deposit of personal property as a security for the performance of an act.
PLEDGEE - The party to whom goods are delivered in pledge.
PLEDGOR - The party delivering goods in pledge.
PLENARY - Full; complete.
POLICE POWER - Inherent power of the state or its political subdivisions to enact laws within constitutional limits to promote the general welfare of society or the community.
POLLING THE JURY - Call the names of persons on a jury and requiring each juror to declare what his verdict is before it is legally recorded.
POST MORTEM - After death.
POWER OF ATTORNEY - A writing authorizing one to act for another.
PRECEPT - An order, warrant, or writ issued to an officer or body of officers, commanding him or them to do some act within the scope of his or their powers.
PRELIMINARY FACT - Fact upon the existence or nonexistence of which depends the admissibility or inadmissibility of evidence. The phrase "the admissibility or inadmissibility of evidence" includes the qualification or disqualification of a person to be a witness and the existence or nonexistence of a privilege.
PREPONDERANCE - Outweighing.
PRESENTMENT - A report by a grand jury on something they have investigated on their own knowledge.
PRESUMPTION - An assumption of fact resulting from a rule of law which requires such fact to be assumed from another fact or group of facts found or otherwise established in the action.
PRIMA FACUE - At first sight.
PRIMA FACIE CASE - A case where the evidence is very patent against the defendant.
PRINCIPAL - The source of authority or rights; a person primarily liable as differentiated from "principle" as a primary or basic doctrine.
PRO AND CON - For and against.
PRO RATA - Proportionally.
PROBATE - Relating to proof, especially to the proof of wills.
PROBATIVE - Tending to prove.
PROCEDURE - In law, this term generally denotes rules which are established by the Federal, State, or local Governments regarding the types of pleading and courtroom practice which must be followed by the parties involved in a criminal or civil case.
PROCLAMATION - A public notice by an official of some order, intended action, or state of facts.

PROFFERED EVIDENCE - The admissibility or inadmissibility of which is dependent upon the existence or nonexistence of a preliminary fact.
PROMISSORY (NOTE) - A promise in writing to pay a specified sum at an expressed time, or on demand, or at sight, to a named person, or to his order, or bearer.
PROOF - The establishment by evidence of a requisite degree of belief concerning a fact in the mind of the trier of fact or the court.
PROPERTY - Includes both real and personal property.
PROPRIETARY (adj.) - Relating or pertaining to ownership; usually a single owner.
PROSECUTE - To carry on an action or other judicial proceeding; to proceed against a person criminally.
PROVISO - A limitation or condition in a legal instrument.
PROXIMATE - Immediate; nearest
PUBLIC EMPLOYEE - An officer, agent, or employee of a public entity.
PUBLIC ENTITY - Includes a national, state, county, city and county, city, district, public authority, public agency, or any other political subdivision or public corporation, whether foreign or domestic.
PUBLIC OFFICIAL - Includes an official of a political dubdivision of such state or territory and of a municipality.
PUNITIVE - Relating to punishment.

Q

QUASH - To make void.
QUASI - As if; as it were.
QUID PRO QUO - Something for something; the giving of one valuable thing for another.
QUITCLAIM (v.) - To release or relinquish claim or title to, especially in deeds to realty.
QUO WARRANTO - A legal procedure to test an official's right to a public office or the right to hold a franchise, or to hold an office in a domestic corporation.

R

RATIFY - To approve and sanction.
REAL PROPERTY - Includes lands, tenements, and hereditaments.
REALTY - A brief term for real property.
REBUT - To contradict; to refute, especially by evidence and arguments.
RECEIVER - A person who is appointed by the court to receive, and hold in trust property in litigation.
RECIDIVIST - Habitual criminal.
RECIPROCAL - Mutual.
RECOUPMENT - To keep back or get something which is due; also, it is the right of a defendant to have a deduction from the amount of the plaintiff's damages because the plaintiff has not fulfilled his part of the same contract.
RECROSS EXAMINATION - Examination of a witness by a cross-examiner subsequent to a redirect examination of the witness.
REDEEM - To release an estate or article from mortgage or pledge by paying the debt for which it stood as security.
REDIRECT EXAMINATION - Examination of a witness by the direct examiner subsequent to the cross-examination of the witness.
REFEREE - A person to whom a cause pending in a court is referred by the court, to take testimony, hear the parties, and report thereon to the court.

REFERENDUM - A method of submitting an important legislative or administrative matter to a direct vote of the people.
RELEVANT EVIDENCE - Evidence including evidence relevant to the credulity of a witness or hearsay declarant, having any tendency in reason to prove or disprove any disputed fact that is of consequence to the determination of the action.
REMAND - To send a case back to the lower court from which it came, for further proceedings.
REPLEVIN - An action to recover goods or chattels wrongfully taken or detained.
REPLY (REPLICATION) - Generally, a reply is what the plaintiff or other person who has instituted proceedings says in answer to the defendant's case.
RE JUDICATA - A thing judicially acted upon or decided.
RES ADJUDICATA - Doctrine that an issue or dispute litigated and determined in a case between the opposing parties is deemed permanently decided between these parties.
RESCIND (RECISSION) - To avoid or cancel a contract.
RESPONDENT - A defendant in a proceeding in chancery or admiralty; also, the person who contends against the appeal in a case.
RESTITUTION - In equity, it is the restoration of both parties to their original condition (when practicable), upon the rescission of a contract for fraud or similar cause.
RETROACTIVE (RETROSPECTIVE) - Looking back; effective as of a prior time.
REVERSED - A term used by appellate courts to indicate that the decision of the lower court in the case before it has been set aside.
REVOKE - To recall or cancel.
RIPARIAN (RIGHTS) - The rights of a person owning land containing or bordering on a water course or other body of water, such as lakes and rivers.

S

SALE - A contract whereby the ownership of property is transferred from one person to another for a sum of money or for any consideration.
SANCTION - A penalty or punishment provided as a means of enforcing obedience to a law; also, an authorization.
SATISFACTION - The discharge of an obligation by paying a party what is due to him; or what is awarded to him by the judgment of a court or otherwise.
SCIENTER - Knowingly; also, it is used in pleading to denote the defendant's guilty knowledge.
SCINTILLA - A spark; also the least particle.
SECRET OF STATE - Governmental secret relating to the national defense or the international relations of the United States.
SECURITY - Indemnification; the term is applied to an obligation, such as a mortgage or deed of trust, given by a debtor to insure the payment or performance of his debt, by furnishing the creditor with a resource to be used in case of the debtor's failure to fulfill the principal obligation.
SENTENCE - The judgment formally pronounced by the court or judge upon the defendant after his conviction in a criminal prosecution.
SET-OFF - A claim or demand which one party in an action credits against the claim of the opposing party.
SHALL and MAY - "Shall" is mandatory and "may" is permissive.
SITUS - Location.
SOVEREIGN - A person, body or state in which independent and supreme authority is vested.
STARE DECISIS - To follow decided cases.

STATE - "State" means this State, unless applied to the different parts of the United States. In the latter case, it includes any state, district, commonwealth, territory or insular possession of the United States, including the District of Columbia.
STATEMENT - (a) Oral or written verbal expression or (b) nonverbal conduct of a person intended by him as a substitute for oral or written verbal expression.
STATUTE - An act of the legislature. Includes a treaty.
STATUTE OF LIMITATION - A statute limiting the time to bring an action after the right of action has arisen.
STAY - To hold in abeyance an order of a court.
STIPULATION - Any agreement made by opposing attorneys regulating any matter incidental to the proceedings or trial.
SUBORDINATION (AGREEMENT) - An agreement making one's rights inferior to or of a lower rank than another's.
SUBORNATION - The crime of procuring a person to lie or to make false statements to a court.
SUBPOENA - A writ or order directed to a person, and requiring his attendance at a particular time and place to testify as a witness.
SUBPOENA DUCES TECUM - A subpoena used, not only for the purpose of compelling witnesses to attend in court, but also requiring them to bring with them books or documents which may be in their possession, and which may tend to elucidate the subject matter of the trial.
SUBROGATION - The substituting of one for another as a creditor, the new creditor succeeding to the former's rights.
SUBSIDY - A government grant to assist a private enterprise deemed advantageous to the public.
SUI GENERIS - Of the same kind.
SUIT - Any civil proceeding by a person or persons against another or others in a court of justice by which the plaintiff pursues the remedies afforded him by law.
SUMMONS - A notice to a defendant that an action against him has been commenced and requiring him to appear in court and answer the complaint.
SUPRA - Above; this word occurring by itself in a book refers the reader to a previous part of the book.
SURETY - A person who binds himself for the payment of a sum of money, or for the performance of something else, for another.
SURPLUSAGE - Extraneous or unnecessary matter.
SURVIVORSHIP - A term used when a person becomes entitled to property by reason of his having survived another person who had an interest in the property.
SUSPEND SENTENCE - Hold back a sentence pending good behavior of prisoner.
SYLLABUS - A note prefixed to a report, especially a case, giving a brief statement of the court's ruling on different issues of the case.

T

TALESMAN - Person summoned to fill a panel of jurors.
TENANT - One who holds or possesses lands by any kind of right or title; also, one who has the temporary use and occupation of real property owned by another person (landlord), the duration and terms of his tenancy being usually fixed by an instrument called "a lease."
TENDER - An offer of money; an expression of willingness to perform a contract according to its terms.
TERM - When used with reference to a court, it signifies the period of time during which the court holds a session, usually of several weeks or months duration.

TESTAMENTARY - Pertaining to a will or the administration of a will.
TESTATOR (male)
TESTATRIX (female) - One who makes or has made a testament or will.
TESTIFY (TESTIMONY) - To give evidence under oath as a witness.
TO WIT - That is to say; namely.
TORT - Wrong; injury to the person.
TRANSITORY - Passing from place to place.
TRESPASS - Entry into another's ground, illegally.
TRIAL - The examination of a cause, civil or criminal, before a judge who has jurisdiction over it, according to the laws of the land.
TRIER OF FACT - Includes (a) the jury and (b) the court when the court is trying an issue of fact other than one relating to the admissibility of evidence.
TRUST - A right of property, real or personal, held by one party for the benefit of another.
TRUSTEE - One who lawfully holds property in custody for the benefit of another.

U

UNAVAILABLE AS A WITNESS - The declarant is (1) Exempted or precluded on the ground of privilege from testifying concerning the matter to which his statement is relevant; (2) Disqualified from testifying to the matter; (3) Dead or unable to attend or to testify at the hearing because of then existing physical or mental illness or infirmity; (4) Absent from the hearing and the court is unable to compel his attendance by its process; or (5) Absent from the hearing and the proponent of his statement has exercised reasonable diligence but has been unable to procure his attendance by the court's process.
ULTRA VIRES - Acts beyond the scope and power of a corporation, association, etc.
UNILATERAL - One-sided; obligation upon, or act of one party.
USURY - Unlawful interest on a loan.

V

VACATE - To set aside; to move out.
VARIANCE - A discrepancy or disagreement between two instruments or two aspects of the same case, which by law should be consistent.
VENDEE - A purchaser or buyer.
VENDOR - The person who transfers property by sale, particularly real estate; the term "seller" is used more commonly for one who sells personal property.
VENIREMEN - Persons ordered to appear to serve on a jury or composing a panel of jurors.
VENUE - The place at which an action is tried, generally based on locality or judicial district in which an injury occurred or a material fact happened.
VERDICT - The formal decision or finding of a jury.
VERIFY - To confirm or substantiate by oath.
VEST - To accrue to.
VOID - Having no legal force or binding effect.
VOIR DIRE - Preliminary examination of a witness or a juror to test competence, interest, prejudice, etc.

W

WAIVE - To give up a right.
WAIVER - The intentional or voluntary relinquishment of a known right.
WARRANT (WARRANTY) (v.) - To promise that a certain fact or state of facts, in relation to the subject matter, is, or shall be, as it is represented to be.

WARRANT (n.) - A writ issued by a judge, or other competent authority, addressed to a sheriff, or other officer, requiring him to arrest the person therein named, and bring him before the judge or court to answer or be examined regarding the offense with which he is charged.

WRIT - An order or process issued in the name of the sovereign or in the name of a court or judicial officer, commanding the performance or nonperformance of some act.

WRITING - Handwriting, typewriting, printing, photostating, photographing and every other means of recording upon any tangible thing any form of communication or representation, including letters, words, pictures, sounds, or symbols, or combinations thereof.

WRITINGS AND RECORDINGS - Consists of letters, words, or numbers, or their equivalent, set down by handwriting, typewriting, printing, photostating, photographing, magnetic impulse, mechanical or electronic recording, or other form of data compilation.

Y

YEA AND NAY - Yes and no.

YELLOW DOG CONTRACT - A contract by which employer requires employee to sign an instrument promising as condition that he will not join a union during its continuance, and will be discharged if he does join.

Z

ZONING - The division of a city by legislative regulation into districts and the prescription and application in each district of regulations having to do with structural and architectural designs of buildings and of regulations prescribing use to which buildings within designated districts may be put.